151

Quick Ideas to Improve Your People Skills

151

Quick Ideas to Improve Your People Skills

Bob Dittmer

and

Stephanie McFarland

151 QUICK IDEAS TO IMPROVE YOUR PEOPLE SKILLS
EDITED BY KARA REYNOLDS
TYPESET BY MICHAEL FITZGIBBON
Cover design by Jeff Piasky
Printed in the U.S.A.

To order this title, please call toll-free 1-800-CAREER-1 (NJ and Canada: 201-848-0310) to order using VISA or MasterCard, or for further information on books from Career Press.

The Career Press, Inc., 220 West Parkway, Unit 12
Pompton Plains, NJ 07444
www.careerpress.com

Library of Congress Cataloging-in-Publication Data
Dittmer, Robert E., 1950–
   151 quick ideas to improve your people skills / by Robert E. Dittmer and Stephanie McFarland.
      p. cm.
      Includes index.
      ISBN 978-1-60163-037-7
   1. Interpersonal communication. 2. Interpersonal relations. I. McFarland, Stephanie, 1968– II. Title. III. Title: One hundred fifty-one quick ideas to improve your people skills.

   BF637.C45D583 2009
   158.2'6--dc22

                                                        2008035812

Contents

How to Use This Book   **13**

Introduction   **15**

1. Why Interpersonal Skills Are So Important   17

2. People Don't Care How Much You Know
   Until They Know How Much You Care   18

3. Social Intelligence vs. Technical Knowledge   19

4. Be Socially Aware   21

5. Relationships Are Priority   22

6. The Nature of Your Relationships   23

7. Envision What You Want From Your Relationships   24

8. Behave in a Way That Secures Relationships   25

9. Look for Ways to Serve Others   26

10. Don't Ingratiate   27

11. Apply the Pygmalion Effect   28

12. Believe That All People Start
    With Good Intentions   29

13. Give 'Em the Benefit of the Doubt   30

14. Live by the Golden Rule 31

15. Practice the Platinum Rule 32

16. Always Look Toward Solutions 33

17. Have Reasonable Expectations of Yourself 34

18. Have Reasonable Expectations of Others 35

19. Be Principle-Centered 36

20. Allow Others to Hold to Their Principles 37

21. Set Boundaries 38

22. Defend Your Boundaries 39

23. Be Genuine 40

24. Don't Take Yourself Too Seriously 41

25. Have a Sense of Humor 42

26. Laugh at Yourself 43

27. Cherish Your Goofs 44

28. Social Skills Are Always a Work in Progress 45

29. Your Character—and Your Reputation—
Is Your Calling Card 46

30. Be Authentic 47

31. Act With Integrity 48

32. Build Trust 49

33. Keep Your Word 50

34. Be Straight Up 51

35. View Discernment as a Gift 52

36. Always Show Respect 53

37. Practice Tolerance   54

38. Choose Words Carefully   55

39. Words: *I* vs. *We*   57

40. Use Kind Words   58

41. Don't Kill Relationships With Your Behavior   59

42. Do Not Gossip   60

43. Don't Be Dismissive   61

44. Don't Be Condescending   62

45. Don't Be Manipulative   63

46. Don't Make Assumptions   64

47. Don't Be Pessimistic   65

48. Don't Be a Cynic   66

49. Don't Be Over-Reactive   67

50. Don't Be Domineering   68

51. Don't Be Overly Opinionated   69

52. Don't Be Overly Aggressive   70

53. Help Others Grow   71

54. Believe in Others   71

55. Wage Peace in Your Relationships   72

56. Be a Peacemaker Between Friends   73

57. Respect Different Personality Types   74

58. Understand Different Styles   75

59. Recognize That Styles Differ From Opinions   76

60. Know Your Own Style   77

61. Stretch Beyond Your Style 78

62. Embrace Different Styles 79

63. Determine if You Are Shy 80

64. Overcome Shyness 81

65. Overcome Feeling Inferior 82

66. Overcome Feeling Intimidated 84

67. Don't Be Too Talkative 85

68. Listen, Don't Talk 86

69. Get Out of Your Own Way 86

70. Douse the Domineering 87

71. Don't Be Reactive 88

72. Tackle the Intimidator 89

73. Strive for Live Interaction 90

74. Practice Face-to-Face Communication 91

75. At Least Make It Live 92

76. Beware of E-mail 93

77. Remember That People Are Creatures of Emotion 94

78. Fill the Emotional Bank Account 95

79. Make Friends 96

80. Develop Your Emotional Intelligence 97

81. Remember Names 98

82. Look 'Em in the Eye 99

83. Give Your Undivided Attention 100

84. Be "Present" 101

85. Practice Good Listening   102

86. Connect With People Through Questions   104

87. Be Careful With Your Opinions   105

88. Withhold Judgment   106

89. See Both Sides   107

90. Edify, Edify, Edify   109

91. Give Honesty With an Equal Dose of Compassion   110

92. Help Others Be Heard   111

93. Help Others Be Understood   112

94. Allow People to Save Face   113

95. Encourage   114

96. Encourage With Words and Perspective   115

97. Pat Others on the Back   117

98. Be a Cheerleader   118

99. Help Others Achieve Their Goals   119

100. Let Others Shine   120

101. Look for Reasons to Celebrate   122

102. Remember Birthdays, Anniversaries, and Such   123

103. Fill Your Own Emotional Bank Account   124

104. Feed Your Own Needs   125

105. Call on Your Support Group   126

106. Keep Honest Company   127

107. Get Inspired   128

108. Find Friends Who Edify You in Your Absence   129

109.   Find a Class Act to Follow   130

110.   Take a "People Break"   131

111.   Sharpen the Saw by Sharpening Your Mind   133

112.   Get Away From Your Desk for Lunch   134

113.   Attend Social Events   135

114.   Handle Conflict With Confidence   136

115.   Can't We All Just Get Along?   137

116.   365 Opportunities for Conflict—
       366 in a Leap Year   138

117.   See Conflict or Disagreement as an Opportunity   140

118.   See Rough Starts as an Opportunity   141

119.   Breathe!   142

120.   Give Yourself a Pep Talk   143

121.   Have the Difficult Conversations Beforehand   144

122.   Handle Conflict One-on-One   145

123.   Having Your Say Doesn't Mean
       Always Having Your Way   146

124.   Learn to Eat Crow   147

125.   Bring the Peace Pipe   148

126.   Break Bread   149

127.   Fight Fair   150

128.   Be Mindful of Your Thoughts;
       They Can Be a Path to the Dark Side   151

129.   Don't Take Things Personally   153

130.   Don't Make Things Personal   154

131. He Who Keeps His Mouth Shut, Keeps His Life   155

132. Dial Down the Volume   156

133. Watch Your Body Language—It Speaks Volumes   157

134. Give People Space   158

135. What Goes Over the Devil's Back, Always Comes Under His Belly   159

136. There Is No Right or Wrong   160

137. Winner Never Takes All   161

138. Fight for the Relationship   162

139. Get Clear   163

140. Present, Don't Persuade   164

141. Ask, Don't Tell   165

142. Look for Middle Ground   166

143. Start From a Point of Commonality   167

144. Some Nuts Are Worth Cracking   168

145. Put the "Moose on the Table"   169

146. Pick Your Battles   170

147. Mend Fences   171

148. Forgive Yourself for Failings   172

149. Forgive Others as Well   174

150. Be the First to Offer the Olive Branch— or the Peace Pipe   175

151. Every Difficult Relationship Has Lessons   176

Index   179

About the Authors   187

How to Use This Book

Every quick idea in this book is tested and true. The ideas come from the collected experiences and wisdom of hundreds of people—well beyond just the authors. And they are presented here to help you learn how to better create lasting relationships with others through improving your people skills.

The book is designed to be consumed piecemeal—that is, in small bites. So don't try all of these ideas at once. Read the book quickly through to gain a quick impression of the ideas here, and then start picking out those that seem to be immediately helpful, and try them out. Some of these ideas are in sequence, and those will make logical sense to you when you read them. Later, routinely go back and review the others, and pick a few more to try. And so on....

Every 90 days or so, revisit this book for some new ideas or techniques. As your situation changes you may well find usable ideas that you discounted earlier.

Remember, all of these ideas and concepts are proven techniques—proven by research and other professionals around the country and around the world. They have worked for others, and they can work for you!

Introduction

Have you ever found yourself saying, "Work would be great if it weren't for the darn people"? Yeah, we've all felt that way from time to time—and, often, more times than we would like. But people are a fact of life, and they are a fact of work. And to be effective in both, you have to learn to deal with them—effectively.

And that's where this book comes in. It is your comprehensive source for building better working—and personal—relationships. Whether you just need to tweak your approach for making connections with people in the workplace, or you're looking for ways to handle an ongoing conflict with a coworker, *151 Quick Ideas to Improve Your People Skills* can help.

The tips and insights shared in this book cover four key areas of people skills: understanding why your social intelligence is critical to your career success, understanding your own interaction style (and how it affects others), how to build goodwill and emotional equity with people, and how to manage conflict—and thrive through it!

For example, you've probably been taught the Golden Rule, but are you familiar with the Platinum Rule? Do you know how powerful the Pygmalion Effect can be in working with people? Do you approach people as creatures of logic, or emotion? Do you know how to set boundaries? Do you have reasonable expectations of *yourself* when dealing with others?

151 Quick Ideas to Improve Your People Skills covers these topics, and much, much more. It gives you a full-spectrum approach to dealing with people in just about every situation—and how to get back on track when you fall off the "people skills" wagon.

In short, this book is an excellent guide, filled with fun, relevant, and practical ideas to which you can relate. So dig in and enjoy! And start learning what it takes to build better working—and personal—relationships.

1

Why Interpersonal Skills Are So Important

A full litany of proverbs exist across continents and cultures that tell us that our interactions with people mean more than anything else we do in this life. In fact, author Daniel Goleman says that our emotional intelligence (EQ) with people is more important than our IQ.

For example, you've probably heard this one: "People don't know how much you know, until they know how much you care." And as the great Dale Carnegie once said: "People are not creatures of logic. They are creatures of emotion."

> ### Assignment
>
> Before you read on, consider the people with whom you interact on a daily or weekly basis, both personally and professionally. What is your relationship with them? Have you carefully cultivated and nurtured those relationships? Do you feel good about those relationships?

Our interactions with people are the signatures of our lives, and that includes our careers, of course—most particularly our work relationships, considering we spend a minimum of eight hours of every day on the job. For us to be effective in our jobs, we have to deal with people, and we have to deal with them *effectively* to be successful in our work. It's one big circular package.

The reward from good working relationships goes beyond the office, too. When we have good relationships at work, it affects the rest of our lives, from how much energy we have when we get home at night to the attitudes we bring home to our families.

People with solid interpersonal skills know how to build effective relationships, and they know that EQ *is* more important than IQ. They know it's the currency that buys more reward in life than any gold coin or greenback ever produced.

Epilogue

Who you know is important, but having a network of solid relationships is even more important. To paraphrase a popular advertisement: You need people.

2

People Don't Care How Much You Know Until They Know How Much You Care

In developing relationships, people first need to care about you. And in order to care about you, they often need to understand that you care about them. After all, relationships need to be reciprocal to be effective.

We see this daily with students at a university where I teach. Students walk into the classroom wanting to have an academic, learning relationship with the professor,

Assignment

Think about your own experiences with others. Do you recognize people with whom you have good, solid relationships that were developed because you discovered they really cared about you? Did that lead you to reciprocate? Do you have other, weak relationships in which you don't sense that the other person really cares?

18

but are often not sure whether the professor really cares about them or is just there to get the lecture in and go back to researching. The good professors find ways to communicate to students early on that they truly care about the students' successes.

Those that do so find students engaging them before and after class, e-mailing them with thoughts and ideas, and doing more than the minimum in class to be successful. It makes for a superb learning environment where everyone benefits—even the professor. The professor benefits by having students engaged and involved, which is much better than having lumps sit in the classroom and merely listen. The students benefit by knowing that the professor is there to be a part of their learning process in a personal way, not just as a role or function.

We've seen many professor/student relationships last years, even after college is done and the student is off to a profession. These students are often great advocates for the university and the programs the professor teaches.

Epilogue

Important and effective relationships are built on a foundation of interest and concern for the other party. If you don't care about them, why should they care about you?

3

Social Intelligence vs. Technical Knowledge

Though we spend the vast majority of our lives developing our technical capabilities to make us attractive in the job market, few of us put specific focus on developing our people skills.

But it is the people skills—also known as social intelligence—that determine our overall long-term success. After all, we don't work in a vacuum; we work with other people, in a myriad of situations and circumstances.

> ### *Assignment*
>
> Using the description of social intelligence given here, rate yourself on each factor and assess how well you measure up. Then make a plan to address any shortcomings.

Think about it for a moment. Just about anyone can learn technical skills associated with his or her area of interest. Add practice to that knowledge and you get technical proficiency. Technical skills require us to understand and implement concepts, theories, and tactical knowledge, such as how to work with a specific business or industrial machine. But these do not have opinions, experiences, values, emotions—the things that make working with people both difficult and rewarding.

Although employers today certainly demand technical proficiency from their employees, they require so much more. They want people who can communicate, show leadership, solve problems, know who they are in terms of strengths and weaknesses, are confident, can adapt and flex with rapidly changing work environments, and have a sense of energy when implementing the day-to-day.

They also want employees who are socially sensitive, know how to build rapport, and influence others in a way that moves themselves and others forward. This takes social intelligence, which means being aware of who you are—the good, the bad, and the ugly. It also means knowing how to manage yourself—your energy, your emotions, and your reactions. And it means having the ability to see things from others' perspectives and build relationships through all kinds of situations.

In short, having technical expertise is not enough. To be successful today, you must be socially intelligent. The good news is that social intelligence is something you can develop and practice every day, and fine-tune throughout your life.

Epilogue

Employers today want employees who are socially sensitive, know how to build rapport, and influence others in a way that moves themselves and others forward.

4

Be Socially Aware

It is important for you to recognize that any good team or effective group of people is dependent on social interactions—both personal and professional. As a consequence, you need to understand that there are always set patterns of interactions that we call *networks*. These networks exist on a formal and informal basis.

Assignment

Look around you. Where are the networks, both formal and informal, and who is in them? Which ones are important to your success? How can you join them?

Formal networks are those established by organizations: networks of employees who work together, who work for specific supervisors, who interact with designated others by their jobs and job descriptions. The organization dictates who interacts with whom.

Informal networks are social in nature, and can be the more important of the two types. These networks are social in that people who interact in these networks are self-selected. They choose with whom they will interact rather than have others, such as an organization, choose for them. Some are in organizations; some are outside organizations. An example is a group of friends from college who meet occasionally to have lunch and exchange life experiences. Or it could be a group of like professionals (CPAs, for example) who meet monthly to talk about their profession.

It is important to recognize these networks, identify those that are important to you, and then become part of those networks.

Epilogue

These social networks are especially important because they set up relationships that can be helpful in the future.

5

Relationships Are Priority

Okay, we've started talking about relationships, and here's why: Your people skills lead to important relationships that can help you in your personal and professional lives.

Assignment

Identify the people with whom you already have relationships in your personal and professional life. Are they good ones? Positive? Helpful to you?

It is personal and professional relationships that make all the difference in hearing about that new job opportunity in another company, or that chance to meet an important person in your profession, or that opportunity to meet someone who could be important to and in your future (a future spouse?).

So we will be continually talking about people skills as they lead to positive and mutually beneficial relationships in your life.

> ### Epilogue
> *Relationships are the social interactions that make societies function effectively. Gain them and maintain them.*

6

The Nature of Your Relationships

When you think of the people around you, particularly at work, think of the level of those relationships. Not all are similarly developed, are they? Some people you have rapport with, some people you're just getting to

> ### Assignment
> Make a list of your key relationships and then determine where they fall on a continuum, from solid rapport to recently introduced.

know, and some relationships fall in the middle.

As you interact with people, you have to remember that relationships are also subject to the situations and circumstances of the moment. How well you handle them together—the nature of the relationship and the current circumstances—determines how well they will progress, or stall.

For example, a key relationship could be fine in the morning, but in the afternoon a poorly handled disagreement could alter that relationship.

If you take stock now of where each of your key relationships stand, you'll be better able to apply the tips and techniques described in the pages ahead. And you'll be able to keep them moving in a positive direction for the future.

> **Epilogue**
> *Knowing the nature of your key relationships will help you know which people strategies are most effective when circumstances bring change.*

7

Envision What You Want From Your Relationships

As you consider the relationships you just listed (in Idea 6), think about where you want to take each relationship. Analyze your list and set relationship goals.

For example, would you like to build a better rapport with someone you just met? Is this someone with whom you will be working on a regular basis, and a stronger rapport will help you both work more effectively?

> ### *Assignment*
> Take your list from Idea 6, and now set goals for each relationship, ranging from three to six months. This will help you remain focused on what you want to achieve as you work through circumstances and situations that can affect the relationship through time.

That's a good goal! That's what we call mutually beneficial—a stronger rapport can help you both. In short, a better acquaintance and some coworker bonding will create a win-win: a situation in which you both gain from the relationship.

And remember: A win-win is always the ultimate relationship goal.

> **Epilogue**
> *Set relationship goals that create a win-win for each party.*

8

Behave in a Way That Secures Relationships

The best way to build and maintain a relationship is to apply both the Golden Rule and the Platinum Rule. One encourages you to treat others as *you* want to be treated, and the other requires that you treat others as *they* want to be treated.

> **Assignment**
> Look more closely at your list of relationships, and what you want from each. Now, what do you need to do to secure those relationships now and through time? Keep reading.

Generally, both fall into two basic categories: respect and trust. If you treat others with respect, a basic tenet of all relationships, they will trust you. And you need to maintain that trust to retain their respect, which means you have to do a lot of things right in every interaction. You have to maintain people's confidences, you have to allow them to save face, and you have to hear them, and let them be heard.

The list is long, and it's focused and tedious work some days (every day with some people). But if you want solid relationships that last, you have to behave in a way that secures them.

> ### Epilogue
> *Securing relationships with people means you have to treat them in ways that demonstrate trust and respect with every interaction.*

9

Look for Ways to Serve Others

Building solid relationships means finding ways to help others, and, in time, you have to let others help you. In short, relationships are a dance of service. To be good with people, you have to firmly adopt a service mentality.

Yet, serving others can be very rewarding, in some simple

> ### *Assignment*
> Look at your list (from Idea 6). How can you serve those people? Once you know, act. Make the offer. Or wait until the time is right or the need has developed.

ways. For example, you can serve others by being a coworker in whom to confide, a friend who inspires people, or an office cheerleader who drives someone to achieve his or her goals. The following pages give you scores of ideas and opportunities to serve others—from helping them to be heard to letting them shine.

Discover what you can do to help those around you. Serving others is a quick way to start a relationship on a positive note, and nurture a developing one.

> ### Epilogue
> Service to others is the strongest binding force in relationships.

10

Don't Ingratiate

We've given this one a nice word in the title; you know it as something else. And by any other word or set of words, it's something that becomes a significant barrier to solid and positive relationships.

Not sure what I mean? Brown-noser. Suck-up. Teacher's pet. These are just some of the words and phrases used for the

> ### Assignment
> Watch others who behave this way. What do you think of them? What is your attitude toward them? It isn't positive, is it? Do you want to be perceived that way? If not, stay away from this behavior.

same thing—there are others inappropriate for this book. None of them suggest a positive relationship.

Instead, one party has the power over the other. And those who recognize that relationship will denigrate you for it. You gain nothing. The person you have ingratiated yourself to thinks less of you. Others recognize it as an attempt to gain undue influence and discount you for it.

Ingratiating yourself with the boss or with others is simply not a positive step to any relationship.

27

> **Epilogue**
> *The ability to ingratiate yourself with others might be a skill, but it's a negative and counterproductive one.*

11

Apply the Pygmalion Effect

What? Isn't that a musical? Well, George Bernard Shaw did base his musical on the concept, but the true credit for this psychological theory actually goes to two scholars and a horse (yes, a horse!) in 1911, and it goes like this: You will get from people what you expect of people.

> **Assignment**
> Think of one coworker with whom you have difficulty, or even your child or spouse. In every interaction, treat him exactly as if he has already become the person you wish him to be. Practice this long enough, and you'll be pleasantly surprised by the results.

In case that description is as clear as mud, we'll let Shaw's character Eliza Doolittle explain it:

"You see, really and truly, apart from the things anyone can pick up (the dressing and the proper way of speaking and so on), the difference between a lady and a flower girl is not how she behaves, but how she's treated. I shall always be a flower girl to Professor Higgins, because he always treats me as a flower girl, and always will. But I know I can be a lady to you because you always treat me as a lady, and always will."

If you believe the best of people, you will treat them as if they are the best. And, in turn, they will likely give you exactly what you believe and expect. That's the Pygmalion Effect, and it's been proven in psychological studies.

Epilogue

Use the Pygmalion Effect to your advantage: Believe the best of people, and expect the best from them.

12

Believe That All People Start With Good Intentions

Repeat after me: "The glass is half full." Don't fall into the trap of assuming everyone has some ulterior motive for everything they do, which is inimical to you and your goals. Be positive and start with the assumption that everyone is operating with good intentions.

Assignment

Examine your approach to people. Do you think well of them until they demonstrate otherwise, or do you automatically assume they are opposed to you? If the latter, consider a change of attitude.

If you assume otherwise, you will be perceived as distrusting. That establishes an internal (and often external) reputation as a skeptic. And that leads to: "If he doesn't trust me, why should I trust him?"

But if you maintain the assumption that all people are working from a point of good intentions—that they mean well—then you release yourself to think the best of people, and expect the best from them in return (see Idea 11). In a sense, you manifest what you think about others. So think positive thoughts about them, always starting from the assumption that they have good intentions, until you have well-founded reasons not to.

> ### Epilogue
> *Most people want to behave appropriately, and do want positive relationships. Assume they mean well.*

13

Give 'Em the Benefit of the Doubt

We are often too quick to judge the actions and motivations of others. When things don't go specifically as they should, we too often look to place blame. We tend to jump to conclusions.

Assignment

Think back on your own experiences. Have you done this to others in the past? Have others done this to you? How did you feel? How did they react?

Instead of looking first to place blame, look to give others the benefit of the doubt. Hold off on thinking someone is the problem until you have established evidence. You want others to do this for you (see the Golden Rule), so do it for others.

This is especially important when evaluating motivations. Don't make assumptions.

> **Epilogue**
> *Giving others the benefit of the doubt allows them to do the same for you. Reciprocal respectful treatment leads to solid relationships.*

14

Live by the Golden Rule

We're sure you remember this one: "Do unto others as you would have them do unto you."

You may have learned this from your father, mother, grandmother, or Sunday School teacher. And it's an adage people across the world embrace as a universal human truth. It means, if you want others to treat you with respect and courtesy, then you have to treat them in the same manner.

> **Assignment**
> Examine your own relationships with others. Are you practicing the Golden Rule? If not, why not?

The beauty of the Golden Rule is that it has no mystique to it—it's straightforward and simple. Treat others as you want to be treated. The rule remains the same whether you're 8 or 80.

> **Epilogue**
> *It's the Golden Rule because it's the ultimate tenet of human relationships.*

15

Practice the Platinum Rule

Now let's learn about the Platinum Rule. Dr. Tony Alessandra gets the credit for this one, a logical companion to the Golden Rule.

Assignment

To find out more about the Platinum Rule, visit *www.platinumrule.com*.

Where the Golden Rule focuses on you, the Platinum Rule focuses on others. The rule states: "Do unto others as they would do unto themselves."

It means it's important to learn how others want to be treated, and then treat them as such.

To practice this rule, you have to observe and listen to others, discover their wants and needs, and then try to meet those needs. In doing so, you create a win-win situation, a mutually beneficial relationship—one that serves both parties with mutual gains.

Epilogue

If you follow the Golden Rule only, you could stumble in some relationships. You must also practice the Platinum Rule.

16

Always Look Toward Solutions

When it comes to relationships, you have look toward solutions that move them forward—and not the problems that keep them stagnant.

Too often we focus on the problems of a relationship, such as people's past transgressions that hurt us, or

> ### *Assignment*
>
> Consider your list from Idea 6 again. Which relationships have you stuck? Keep reading to learn how to move them forward.

workplace pettiness. Always focusing on the problems we have with people can make us stuck, sometimes so much that we can appear bitter.

You have to get past this if you want your relationships to grow and become what you envision them to be. Of course, life will give you lots of practice because ever-changing situations and circumstances throw us curve balls all the time, and that keeps our relationships in motion.

The goal is to look for solutions that move your relationships in the right direction, in a way that deepens respect, trust, and camaraderie.

Epilogue

When it comes to cultivating your relationships, you have to focus on solutions that keep them moving forward.

17

Have Reasonable Expectations of Yourself

Know thyself. A key to being socially intelligent is being self aware. Do you have a reasonable understanding of yourself? Do you know what sets you off? Do

> ### Assignment
>
> Referring to your list (Idea 6), jot down what expectations you have for moving each relationship forward. Are your expectations of yourself realistic?

you know what calms you down? Do you know your interpersonal strengths and weaknesses?

As you attempt to take relationships to new places, make sure you have reasonable expectations of yourself. For example, if you struggle with feelings of inferiority, it might not be a good idea to try charming the office bully at this point in your life.

You do want to stretch yourself in moving relationships forward, but reaching too far out of your comfort zone can damage your self-confidence. And your self-confidence is an important element of relationship building.

Epilogue

As you attempt to take relationships to new places, make sure you have reasonable expectations of yourself.

18

Have Reasonable Expectations of Others

It's also important to have reasonable expectations of others around you. For example, can you expect the person with whom you've just started working to take direct criticism from you? Probably not. You might need to develop a stronger rapport so this person knows—at an emotional level—that your criticism is constructive and well-meant.

> **Assignment**
>
> Take inventory of your key office relationships and develop a set of reasonable expectations for each of those people.

Having unrealistic expectations of others can lead to failures, disappointments, and hurt feelings. And those always result in damaged relationships.

Just as you should have realistic expectations of yourself, you also need to have reasonable expectations of others.

Epilogue

Having unrealistic expectations of others can lead to damaged or failed relationships.

19

Be Principle-Centered

Here we draw from author Stephen Covey's *Principle-Centered Leadership*, which says that our principles should be the bedrock of our actions and the central driver of how we interact in relationships.

Have you thought about what principles influence you on a daily basis?

> ### *Assignment*
>
> Take some time to reflect on your principles. To what principles do you subscribe, and how do you act in relation to them? Do your actions show you are a principle-centered individual?

Perhaps you should, because in many ways your actions reflect your principles. And the perceptions those actions give will send out a signal to people indicating whether your principles align with theirs.

For example, do you treat others fairly, with integrity and honesty? These are basic principles that people expect us to follow, and they're absolutely essential to building positive relationships.

Yet principles are more than just actions. They're your moral GPS system, so to speak; they guide your decisions and your resulting actions. And they act as an interpersonal beacon for others—telling them who you truly are.

Epilogue

Principle-centered behaviors clearly communicate to others who and what we are.

20

Allow Others to Hold to Their Principles

While you have your own set of principles, recognize that everyone else has a set of principles that guide their decisions and actions, too. Recognize that their principles are, to them, every bit as valid as yours are to you—even though they might be different from yours.

> ### *Assignment*
>
> Think about your principles. How can others think differently from the way you do? Why is that all bad? Can you live with those positions?

You may be pro-life. Others might be pro-choice. You are both operating on a set of principles that are immediately and personally valuable to each of you.

Don't disparage others for their principles. If you disagree, that's okay. But respectfully acknowledge that others think differently than you do, and that their thoughts and their principles are also based on deeply held values and personal convictions.

Recognize, too, that people with different sets of principles and values can still work, live, and play alongside each other quite effectively—if we simply acknowledge and respect others' principles.

Don't let differing principles stand in the way of potential relationships unless you simply cannot live with the opposite view of something. Believe me: This situation is much more rare than you think.

> **Epilogue**
> Remember: Others' principles may be different from yours, but they are also based on deeply held values and personal convictions.

21

Set Boundaries

Setting boundaries is healthy; we all need to set our parameters of what we will accept and what we will not. You shouldn't have to allow all manner of behavior just because you want to create or maintain a relationship. Some behaviors are just not acceptable.

> **Assignment**
> Take some time to think about principles, behaviors, and issues around which you want to place boundaries. You might even want to make a list.

In fact, your principles will usually dictate what your boundaries are. And when you determine what your boundaries are, stick with them! For example, is foul language unacceptable to you? Are there certain topics you feel are off-limits in some relationships? Are politics and religion two things you won't discuss at work?

These are only a few of many areas where you might feel the need to set boundaries. And if so, then do so. Remember: Boundaries provide predictability for others about what is appropriate in their relationships with you, and they help set expectations for all parties.

> **Epilogue**
> *You should have boundaries to make your personal interactions with others appropriate to you. You'll find others have them, too, and will appreciate yours.*

22

Defend Your Boundaries

Once you have set your boundaries, vigorously and consistently defend them. Once you start allowing exceptions, you remove the predictability from acceptable behaviors, and people will be left wondering what is appropriate.

> **Assignment**
> Think through some ways to defend boundaries without attacking others.

If you have a boundary established about the use of four-letter words in conversation at work, stick with it. If you let others use that kind of language around you, you let them violate your boundaries on that behavior, and you make them wonder when it is and is not appropriate. You remove the predictability from the situation, making everyone uncomfortable.

You don't have to attack anyone who might be behaving inappropriately. Just ask them to stop, politely. Explain why. Be personal and respectful. But do defend your boundary.

Epilogue
Boundaries lead to predictability, and predictability leads to solid foundations for relationships.

23

Be Genuine

Just be yourself. You've heard that before, haven't you? Well, it's true. People know when you are acting, when you are trying to be someone or some-

---

Assignment

Think about others who have not been genuine, those phonies we all run into. Take a look at the relationships they have—or don't have.

---

thing you are not. You have even met people like that and recognized them for what they are: the guy who says he's really supportive of you or your program, but says otherwise to people behind your back, or the gal who acts as though she knows everyone who is important, and then you find out she's just "blowing smoke."

When you are not genuine, when you are acting a part or role that is not really you, people will recognize that fact. Perhaps not initially or even quickly, but eventually they will know. When that happens, you lose credibility and respect, and relationships are damaged. And it takes a long time to recover from that. Some people never do.

It just pays to be yourself. Say what you believe. Represent yourself and your feelings honestly. Present only what you know, not what you'd like to know.

> **Epilogue**
> *Be genuine. People will respect you for it.*

24

Don't Take Yourself Too Seriously

Life, work, and relationships are important, and require serious attention. But don't be so serious about everything that you can't laugh, smile, or be

> **Assignment**
>
> Inventory your attitudes at work. Are you too serious? Do you need to lighten up a little? Or are you one of those people others like to be around?

happy. If you take yourself too seriously, others will begin to look at you as someone with whom they have to do business, but not someone they want to be around regularly.

You know people like this. Take Frank, for example. He takes everything so seriously that he never cracks a smile, never tells a joke, never lightens up enough to talk about the ballgame over the weekend or the things his kids are doing in school. He's always on task, focused on the mission, business all the time. He's a likable guy, but he's so intense that most people can only take him in small doses. He's just no fun to be around!

Don't be that way. Be one of those people you want to be around.

> **Epilogue**
> *People like others with whom they enjoy interacting regularly. Be one of those people.*

25

Have a Sense of Humor

People with a sense of humor are much more fun to be around than those without. Don't you wish you could spend some time hanging out with Robin Williams, or George Carlin (RIP)?

People with a sense of humor are much more interesting and fun to be around in all walks of life.

> **Assignment**
>
> Learn where you can be humorous comfortably. If telling jokes is not your style, think about funny stories—and share them!

So feel free to crack a joke, laugh, or recount something you may have heard on TV or from the morning drive-time radio. It humanizes you. But don't force it, and don't overdo it. If you force a sense of humor you don't really have, people will recognize that. If you overdo it, you risk the impression that you are not serious enough. Find a happy medium.

> ### Epilogue
>
> *Laughter is a universal magnet that binds people together and helps to create and maintain lasting relationships.*

26

Laugh at Yourself

Self-deprecation is a sort of humor in which people make jokes about themselves, their short-coming, or their mistakes. It's laughing at yourself without concern for damage to your own self-esteem.

> ### *Assignment*
>
> Think about ways you can laugh at yourself—and invite others to do so as well.

For example, we warm up to people who can say about themselves, "Yes, I've been very successful, thanks to sheer dumb luck!"

These kinds of statements also demonstrate an important trait for likability: humility. Humble people are more likable than arrogant people. Really! We've all heard about "that arrogant SOB," but what about "that humble SOB"?

Laughing at yourself makes you human, and that makes you approachable—a good trait to show. So find opportunities to laugh at yourself with others. Let them laugh with you. Just remember that they are laughing *with* you, not *at* you.

> ### Epilogue
> *People would much rather be around someone with the humility to laugh at herself than someone who is arrogant.*

27

Cherish Your Goofs

We all make mistakes.

Cherish mistakes as opportunities. First, view them as an opportunity to apologize. If you make a mistake with someone, the best remedy is a quick and honest apology. An honest apology after a mistake is almost always well received by the other party, and serves to demonstrate your willingness to not only recognize when you are wrong, but also to take responsibility for the mistake.

Assignment

Identify social goofs you have made in the past, and analyze what you did, how it affected the other person, and how you rectified it (or failed to). Then examine the nature of the relationship after the goof. Learn from those experiences.

Second, it is a learning opportunity. Learn what you said or did that offended someone. Or learn what behavior bothered him. Then, having experienced it once, don't do it again. Make it part of what you know about that other person. These revealing moments help solidify your relationships because they often expose you to parts of personalities not always seen by others—both of your personality and the other person's.

> **Epilogue**
> *We all make goofs. The important point is to take responsibility for them and learn from them.*

28

Social Skills Are Always a Work in Progress

Your ability to interact with people, individually and in groups, is an ongoing education. We continually learn our professions and trades throughout the years we work in them,

> **Assignment**
>
> Keep learning and improving your relationship skill set. Study people and their behaviors. Stay on top of communication and language trends, and even fads.

just as we continually learn more about working and interacting with people the more we do it—which is all our lives.

Almost no one ever really becomes an expert at this. People change, different generations have significant differences in interactions and backgrounds, and we learn from our mistakes and our successes—and the mistakes and successes of others.

So always be a student of people and relationship-building. Always look for ways to improve your relationship skill set. Never assume that you've got it down and are now an expert. Once you do that, you'll get a nasty surprise as someone comes up with a new behavior or concern you've never seen before.

Older generations need to continually learn about the relationship rules with younger generations (got teenagers?). And younger generations need to be aware that older generations are different, and that their relationship expectations may be different as a result (got grandparents?).

Epilogue

Learning about people and relationships should never stop. Relationships are dynamic activities, and, recognizing that people change in time, you need to adapt to those changes.

29

Your Character—and Your Reputation—Is Your Calling Card

Your business card is a useful item: It identifies you at that first meeting. After that, it probably does you no good at all. It might not even survive the day.

Assignment

Consider the times you have met someone and he already knew something about you. That's reputation at work.

But your *actions* at a first meeting, and all subsequent communication and behavioral interactions you have with others, establish your reputation as to what kind of person you are. And word gets around; others will know about you even if they have never met you.

"Say, aren't you that guy who works with John in the accounting office?" Ever hear something similar to that when meeting someone new? That's a signal. She already knows something about you from word of mouth. And that word of mouth has already established your initial reputation with that person, and set up an expectation for the relationship that is about to be developed.

It might be right, and it might not. It all depends on what other people have to say about you—that's what your reputation is based upon. So always remember that every relationship you have, for good or for ill, will help establish your reputation with others you may not even have met. So, every relationship is important. All of them. Work at them. See them as valuable to your future.

Epilogue

Reputation is your presence in the relationship market-place. It can make you if you work at solid, positive relationships, or break you if you ignore those relationships.

30

Be Authentic

If you want people to trust you, you have to keep it real. That means you have to own up to who *you* are—and you have to like it.

No one is perfect. We all have flaws. But so many people spend time trying to make us believe they're flaw*less*. You've met them: the know-it-all, the embellisher, the goodie-two-shoes. The list goes on.

It takes a lot of energy to hide our faults and pretend to be something more than we are. And that's a lot of wasted effort. Think about it for a moment: If you're presenting yourself in some form of false light, then you're developing a false reality. In time, you'll be found out.

> ### *Assignment*
> Think about times when you've felt as though you needed to appear as more than you are. How did you feel about yourself? Did it take a lot of energy to keep up the pretense? Then think about the times when you were able to be completely honest about who you are. Did you feel stronger, more courageous, and honest? Give these two situations some thought, and then look for ways to live up to who you really are.

Real relationships are based on the reality of our true character, values, principles, strengths, and weaknesses. In other words, "putting it out there." When we own who we are with modesty and honesty, we can actually relax and begin to feel safe in the fact that people who like us, genuinely like us *just the way we are.*

And that sets you up to attract friends and confidantes whom you can trust. In short, it's reaping what you sow. If you sow authenticity, you'll reap it as well. Standing firmly in the center of who you are is a true demonstration of strength.

> ### Epilogue
> *Keep it real. Be authentic.*

31

Act With Integrity

Acting with integrity is a simple concept to understand. We wrote earlier about operating within a set of principles (see Idea 19).

These principles are based on your personal values. Your behaviors should, then, conform consistently to those principles. If your principles are clear, and you act according to those principles consistently, then you have integrity.

The key here is consistency. Having integrity means behaving in predictable ways based on your principles. As others learn your principles by observing your actions, they will begin to expect certain behaviors of you. That provides predictability and it also indicates to people that you have a clear set of principles on which you base all your actions.

> ### Assignment
>
> Take stock of your principles again. Commit to acting according to those principles. Reflect on your recent actions to ensure that you are doing so.

Epilogue

People who act with integrity are respected, sought after, and successful.

32

Build Trust

Trust is essential to any good relationship. Trust is defined by the Merriam-Webster dictionary as "assured reliance on the character, ability, strength, or truth of someone or something," and "one in which confidence is placed."

You want to have others trust you. That means they need to rely upon you and what you do and say. Similar to integrity, trust is an integral part of your reputation. If you are trustworthy, that means you do what you say and say what you do.

> **Assignment**
>
> Find opportunities to demonstrate your trustworthiness. The more you demonstrate trustworthiness, the more people will place trust in you.

Others will place confidence in people who are trustworthy. If you are trusted, people will have the confidence to work with you and know you will be part of the team, that you will do what you say you will do, that you will act as you say you will act.

How do you build trust? By being trustworthy. Say what you will do, and do what you say you will do. Trust is built on experience with you. It doesn't happen overnight, but rather in time and trial as you consistently demonstrate that you can be trusted.

And trust, as we have already said, is a strong basis for good relationships.

> **Epilogue**
> *Trust is built upon trustworthy actions.*

33

Keep Your Word

Keeping your word is the bedrock of relationships. You must do as you have told people you will do. If you make a promise to do something, do it. Don't pass it off on someone else. You made the promise, you keep the promise!

Sometimes this is painful, or time consuming, or difficult, or challenging, or, or, or.... But it is critically important that you keep your word to others. You will be judged by your reliability. If you can't do it, don't promise it.

> ### Assignment
> Concentrate on keeping your word. Make sure you only promise what you can deliver, and deliver on what you promise.

Nothing damages your relationships with others more than not keeping your word. This is the physical manifestation of trust. If you don't keep your word, you can't be trusted. If you can't be trusted, people will be reluctant to maintain a relationship with you.

> ### Epilogue
> *You will be judged by your willingness to do what you say you will do.*

34

Be Straight Up

Yes, that sounds like a cliché, doesn't it? But it's not. Being straight up means being honest and forthright—but always with compassion (see Idea 91).

> ### Assignment
> Practice being straight up. Read Idea 91.

That means telling people—those who ask—what you *really* think. Not rudely, crudely, or meanly, but in a constructive way.

People actually appreciate honest, straightforward views, even if they differ from their own. In fact, people *respect* those who are constructively "straight up." We often feel we can trust them, because they will tell us what they really think, and not just what they think we want to hear.

As long as what you say is respectful and shared with sensitivity, a straightforward conversation can strengthen your relationship.

Epilogue
Being straight up is helpful to others when done tactfully.

35

View Discernment as a Gift

It's true that not everyone is discerning; it's a difficult trait that is a real challenge to develop. If you have it, cherish it and use it.

Oh, you want to know what it is? Okay.

Assignment

Practice this by doing it. Engage in actively learning about the people around you with whom you want a relationship.

Discernment is the ability to see what is not evident or clearly obvious. Discernment can apply easily to people: If you are discerning, that means you are a good judge of character in others, or a good judge of someone's motivations for doing or not doing something.

You can also think of discernment as accurately perceiving others' actions and motivations. People do things and sometimes you don't know why. If you are truly discerning, you can sense their motivations. The ability to do this comes with experience and a real effort to get to know the other person.

You can also think of discernment as insight. Having insight into how people might react or behave in certain situations is extremely valuable. Again, however, the ability to do this comes with experience and real effort to get to know and understand other people as individuals.

Work at developing this facility. Get to know people and why they do—or don't do—things. Learn what motivates them. Learn what drives them. Once you know those things, you will have discernment.

Epilogue

You become discerning through experience and knowledge about other people.

36

Always Show Respect

Aretha Franklin sang it clearly—R-E-S-P-E-C-T! We all want it, we all expect it, and we all deserve it. No matter who we are or what role we play in any organization, we want respect from others. Indeed, we have a right to expect it. But that means we also need to show others respect.

Assignment

Do it. Treat others the way you want to be treated, with respect. Think about it as you deal and work with others. Are you behaving as you would want them to behave?

This doesn't mean we should ignore problems, overlook shoddy efforts, or disregard inappropriate behavior. But it does mean that we should be treating others with the same respect we would ask them to use in their dealings with us.

Oh, wait. Does this sound familiar? Yep. The Golden Rule (revisit Idea 14).

Epilogue

Remember that it always starts with you. You set the tone for your relationships with others by your behavior toward them.

37

Practice Tolerance

When we speak of tolerance, we are talking about tolerance for other people's points of view, others' ideas, others' strengths and weaknesses, and so on.

Remember that people are all different and they have different attitudes, opinions, and values. They also have different strengths and weaknesses.

Assignment

Practice this the next time someone else comes up short on an assignment or expresses the, "that's the dumbest idea I've ever heard" type of thought.

Sometimes some or all of these things can seem to be a problem. Sometimes they seem to be barriers to relationships and to getting things done.

We all need to recognize that we are different, and to cherish those differences. After all, if we were all the same, it would be a boring world!

Recognize that everyone has a right to their opinions and values, even if they disagree with yours. Agree to disagree, and move forward with your tasks.

The key tolerance you need to develop is for those people who don't have the skills or knowledge you do. Someone makes a mistake because she is not as good at something as you are. Don't fly off the handle; that will surely damage any relationship you may have with her. Work with her. Understand her shortcomings and offer to help her overcome those shortcomings in knowledge or skills. After all, you want her to tolerate your shortcomings, don't you?

Epilogue
We all need a little tolerance for differences and weaknesses in order to create successful working relationships.

38

Choose Words Carefully

Words can kill! Choose the wrong words and they can kill a relationship.

In fact, words have two meanings: denotation and connotation. Denotation is easy: the definition of the word. We learn those in school. Connotations, however, are the real-world emotional responses some words can bring about. Connotation is the concepts

Assignment
Make an inventory of emotionally charged words and phrases, and consciously begin to eliminate that language—those words—from your vocabulary.

and ideas that come to mind when the word is spoken, which are sometimes rooted in its definition, and sometimes not.

Some words are deadly in and of themselves. You would never consider using the "n" word for any reason to anyone. Its definition and connotation are so negative that it evokes strong reactions from just about everyone.

Some words, however, come with an intense emotional charge that goes beyond their definitions. Words such as *stupid, dumb, ignorant,* and general profanity are all pretty obvious. Often we find ourselves using these emotionally charged words in moments of stress, anger, or frustration. And some have made their way into our everyday office speech. For example, many people bristle at the phrase "dumb it down," which clearly communicates that you think you're higher on the intelligence food chain than those around you.

When in the company of people with known special interests or concerns, avoid words to which you know they will react negatively. For example, it's not a good idea to use the word *shyster* when talking to your company's legal counsel. It's also a bad idea to use the phrase *spin doctor* when talking to your public-relations professionals. *Spin doctor* implies lying and deceit, and it's a dirty word in the PR profession.

Be conscious of words so that your interactions can remain on a neutral and common ground. And never try to set someone off emotionally using words. That's manipulative (see Idea 45).

Epilogue
Using the wrong words can significantly damage relationships.

39

Words: I vs. We

In our daily lives, and in our daily interactions with other people, we generally find ourselves using a lot of pronouns: *I, me, we, they, them, he, she,* and so on. And generally there's no problem using them. They serve as a sort of shorthand in spoken and written language that simplifies our communication. Very useful.

However, one of them can be damaging to relationships when overused. That's the pronoun *I*. Here's the problem with *I*: It implies a focus on yourself. If used occasionally and sparingly, it's no problem. However, if used constantly, it leaves people with the impression that the speaker (or writer) is focused only on what the speaker wants, not what others may want.

We see this constantly when teaching students to write cover letters for their resumes when job hunting. They want to communicate that they have the skills and abilities to do the job for which they are applying, but in doing so, they use far too many *I*s, and communicate that they are focused on themselves, not the job or the company.

We see it in small group discussions too. One or more people will constantly express, "Well, I think...," or "I would like to see...," or "I expect that...." This all too often results in group members feeling as though the person speaking is only focused on his perspective, and not interested in others.

A much better word is *we*. Especially in group discussions, *we* connotes a group focus, not an individual focus as does *I*. *We* says, "I'm in this with everyone else and I want to support the group outcome." At the same time, it allows everyone to express their opinions, points of view, ideas, and information in a neutral, group-focused approach.

Epilogue

I *equals me; we equals us.*

40

Use Kind Words

Being positive is always a bridge to good relationships. Part of being positive is using words that communicate kindness. Expressions of congratulations when due are

> **Assignment**
>
> Think about the times people have been kind to you in conversations. Start practicing the same behaviors.

always bridge-builders, as are expressions of condolence when sad personal events take place.

When making observations about someone's performance, use positive words. Be honest about the performance, but be kind about how you express the actions and the remedies.

When observing opinions and reacting to others' statements, positive and kind words are always well received; rarely are negative and critical words.

What are kind words? "Congratulations. I'm sorry. Well done! Great! Super job. Good work; let's examine the situation and work out how we can do better in the future."

Epilogue
Kind words build bridges in relationships.

41

Don't Kill Relationships With Your Behavior

Some behaviors can destroy relationships with other people. Dr. Howard Lambert calls these the Four Horsemen of the Apocalypse. They are behaviors that, if practiced regularly, seriously damage or destroy relationships—or block any chance at having one.

Assignment

Have you practiced any of the Four Horsemen? If so, examine the circumstances and resolve not to do so in the future.

His horsemen are: criticism versus complaint; contempt; defensiveness; and stonewalling. Let's examine each briefly.

Criticism versus Complaint. Lambert notes that a complaint is okay, because it addresses a single issue or behavior. People recognize a complaint as just that, an individual issue. But all too often what is expressed is global criticism that is meant to apply

59

across the board. A complaint is "you missed the deadline on that proposal." Okay, fair enough. A criticism is "you always miss your deadlines." That's global and far-reaching—and may not be true.

Contempt. We often express contempt with condescension and negative facial expression such as a sneer, or with the use of sarcasm. It is almost never helpful in moving a relationship forward positively; it makes the other person feel attacked.

Defensiveness. When you get defensive about something, you are trying to pass responsibility onto others. Defensiveness is an avoidance of responsibility. It says, the problem is not with me, it's with someone else.

Stonewalling. This is tuning someone else out of the conversation. Stonewalling stops the communication. Often this happens in arguments and strong disagreements. Someone stonewalls the issue by tuning out. This effectively stymies any attempt at resolution. No communication—no relationship.

Epilogue
Beware the Four Horsemen!

42

Do Not Gossip

Let's be clear: Gossip is creating rumors and innuendo about other people's professional or personal lives that may or may not be true.

Gossiping about other people, whether true or untrue, leads to misinformation—intentionally or not. And when it does, it is incredibly damaging to that person.

If you engage in repeating rumors and stories you hear from others, you do so at the risk of spreading disinformation and misinformation. Stay away from gossip. Don't do it, and don't stick around when others do it.

> **Assignment**
> Think back to times when others have gossiped about you and it came to your attention. Were you happy about that?

Remember: People almost always find out who spread gossip. When that happens, and if you were involved, your relationship with that person will be seriously damaged.

Epilogue
Gossip. Bad stuff. Stay away.

43

Don't Be Dismissive

Being dismissive is making someone feel as though she is not worthy of your time or attention. It's belittling her by ignoring her. It's saying, perhaps in words and perhaps by behavior, that her thoughts and ideas don't matter.

> **Assignment**
> Recall times when someone has treated you dismissively. Remember how that made you feel?

If you have ever been treated this way, then you know that being dismissed as accounting for nothing is a terrible feeling. It's demeaning and makes you feel as though you are worth less than others. You're depressed, and then, often, angry at the person who treated you that way.

Is this any way to establish a relationship? Of course not. You don't want to be treated this way, and neither do others. If you treat others dismissively, then prepare to have weak or even hostile relationships with them.

Epilogue

Treating people dismissively is more likely to create enemies than friends.

44

Don't Be Condescending

Condescending behaviors are those that result from a patronizing, superior attitude. Patronizing behaviors are those that seem polite and positive on the surface, but are clearly intended to express someone's superiority over you. He expresses ideas or responses that clearly suggest that he is better

Assignment

Think about some of the times people have been condescending to you. Did you appreciate it? What did you think about the person who did it to you?

then you are, or more knowledgeable, or—well, want some examples? Here you go:

"Thanks for your thoughts. We are all refreshed by your unique point of view."

"That's an excellent idea, but I don't know what it has to do with what we are talking about."

"Let me see if I can put that in terms others can understand."

These behaviors can be damaging, and really have no place in your interactions with others. Instead, choose behaviors that build collaboration and trust (revisit ideas 36 and 40).

Epilogue
Condescension leads to destructive relationships.

45

Don't Be Manipulative

Trying to manipulate people is an effort to get them to do something they really don't want to do. When you manipulate someone, you attempt to get her to fall to your agenda by unethical means. That can be by threatening, intimidating, lying, or some other nasty behavior.

Bribery is one way. And it's not always money; it can be favoritism, implied rewards, or the threat (as in coercion) of negative consequences. Use of these techniques results in one party having power over the other. This is known as a win-lose, and that's not a mutually beneficial relationship.

Using manipulative behavior, you might get your way once or twice, but it will always come back to haunt you.

Assignment

To learn more about what manipulative behavior can do for your career, read Idea 135.

Epilogue

Manipulating others is unethical and leads to negative relationships.

46

Don't Make Assumptions

Do you know what *assume* spells? Assumptions make an *ass* of *u* and *me*.

Assumptions are dangerous, yet we make them all the time. We assume that other people know something. We assume that others are in agreement with us without ever asking them. We assume that someone has the skills to do

Assignment

We're sure you've done this in the past. So analyze that circumstance and think about how it might have turned out better if you had avoided the assumption and just asked.

something. We assume that people want the same things we do.

We base these assumptions not on hard evidence, but upon guesses, things others say, and partial information.

Have you ever spoken with someone and assumed he agreed with your position or idea, only to be surprised when he expressed the opposite view? If you do this in front of others, as in a group meeting, you risk damaging your relationship with that person. Worse, others will recognize you made an assumption, and the knowledge will damage your relationship with them.

Avoid making assumptions about anyone or anything. If you don't know for certain, ask.

Epilogue
Assume *spells bad news.*

47

Don't Be Pessimistic

If you are a pessimist, you have a negative expectation of every outcome. You're gloomy and depressing to be around. You always expect that the worst will happen.

Assignment
Examine your behavior. Are you always negative? If so, heal thyself. It's simple: The glass is really half full.

People tend to avoid pessimists, who often gain a reputation for being overly critical and negative. They are not fun to be around. Their pessimism creates a barrier that others either can't penetrate or don't want to bother to.

It's hard to create a positive relationship with a pessimist.

So, always to be an optimist, or at least neutral.

> **Epilogue**
> *Pessimists are depressing to be around.*

48

Don't Be a Cynic

Okay, you think pessimists are bad? Cynics are worse!

A cynic distrusts everyone and everything. A cynic assumes the worst, *always*.

> **Assignment**
>
> Identify cynical attitudes in others, and watch how others respond to them.

Worse, a cynic is very vocal about it.

Cynics are difficult people. They are verbal pessimists. They not only assume the worst, but they also tell you about it in no uncertain terms: "That will never work," "You will never get him to agree to that," "This company will never achieve that goal."

And often they are sarcastic and nasty about it: "You're out of your mind," "If you think that can happen, you come from a different planet," "You've been around her long enough to know we will never be successful."

Wow! Talk about negative vibes!

> **Epilogue**
> *Cynics are verbal pessimists, and people avoid them.*

49

Don't Be Over-Reactive

Sometimes things do not go as planned. Sometimes bad things happen. When they do, don't overreact to them.

Take Jim, for example. He would blow up, yelling and scream-

> **Assignment**
>
> Identify people in your life or past who overreact to things. Do you like it when they do it? Do you avoid them? Do *you* overreact? Well then, take a look at Idea 71.

ing at everyone, especially the person who brought him the bad news. He would go on for an hour. It made for an ugly work situation until he calmed down. Then he was fine. But that hour—wow!

So what happened? People started avoiding the prospect of bringing him bad news. The result? Things festered and got worse.

If you overreact to things, especially bad news, people are going to start avoiding you. This reduces your effectiveness. It reduces your interactions. It creates fear in subordinates and coworkers, and destroys relationships.

> ### Epilogue
> People avoid those who overreact, making relationships difficult.

50

Don't Be Domineering

A domineering person is one who always wants to be in charge.

Consider some of the synonyms for domineering: authoritarian,

Assignment

For thoughts on how to be less domineering, take a look at Idea 70.

dictatorial, overbearing, autocratic, bossy, dominating, high-and-mighty, bullying, high-handed, tyrannical.

Whoa! Do you like that kind of person? Do you like hanging out with someone who is domineering, bossy, and bullying? I doubt it. So don't do it yourself.

Instead, be open to consultation, discussion, and group exploration. Allow others to express their thoughts and opinions. And listen.

Epilogue
Domineering personalities tend not to have positive relationships with others.

51

Don't Be Overly Opinionated

It's not that you should not have opinions; it's just that you should avoid forcing them on others at every opportunity. Allow others to have their own opinions.

Another way to look at this is to find that person—yes, you know one—who lets you know his opinion on ev-erything all the time. He usually doesn't even wait to be asked his opinion, and he expresses it vociferously and with emotion. Often, it's done with the attitude and assumption that other opinions are irrelevant.

> ### Assignment
>
> Examine your own be-haviors. Are you overly opin-ionated? Do you force your opinions on others? Perhaps you need to rein in those opinions a little.

As a consequence, overly opinionated people tend to be avoided. If they are avoided, they also don't get much opportunity to create solid relationships.

Epilogue

Those who are overly opinionated are also often avoided.

52

Don't Be Overly Aggressive

Being aggressive is akin to being dominating. It's taking charge too often and too energetically without allowing others a role or input in the decision or situation. When you are being aggressive, you are only interested in satisfying your own objectives and concerns, and are not interested in others. If fact, aggressive people tend to ignore the interests of others.

> ### *Assignment*
>
> Are you too aggressive with others? If so, take a look as Ideas 77 through 79 for some ideas to adjust your behaviors.

As you can guess, being aggressive is not conducive to building good relationships with other people.

Being *assertive* is much more acceptable, and powerful in building relationships. Assertive behaviors simply ensure that one's opinions or ideas get expressed. But assertive people don't try to dominate the process, and they certainly don't ignore others. Assertive people are, similar to those in a good relationship, looking for a mutually beneficial outcome.

Epilogue

Be assertive, not aggressive.

53

Help Others Grow

All right, this one's simple. People like others who help them. They appreciate others who are aiding them in their profession, on their job, or in their personal lives. If you help someone grow in life, you are part of a very positive relationship.

> **Assignment**
>
> Look for ways to help others become better, more effective, more knowledgeable, more capable, more....

If you help someone at work by showing her new skills, processes, or providing new information and knowledge, you are helping her become better at her job. If you help someone at work by giving him the opportunity to do things he has never done before, or new responsibilities he can grow with, you have participated in his future success.

Epilogue

Giving of yourself to help others is a powerful relationship-builder.

54

Believe in Others

When people know that you believe in them, that you are in their camp, when you are truly supportive of them and want them to succeed, they always do better. Conversely, when people don't think you believe in them, they perform badly.

This is a simple management principle that should also

```
┌─────────────────────────────┐
│   Assignment                │
│   Read ideas 92 through     │
│ 99.                         │
└─────────────────────────────┘
```

be applied to personal and professional relationships. The more you believe in others, and express that belief, the better they will do and the stronger your relationship will be with them. (Think back to the Pygmalion Effect in Idea 11.)

How do you express belief? In simple comments and behaviors. Start by being encouraging. Tell them you care and want them to succeed. When they have successes, congratulate them. When they have failures, help them improve and overcome. When they need help, provide it. Be there for them if they have questions or need assistance. Say yes.

The more you demonstrate that you truly believe in someone else, the stronger the positive relationship you are building with that person.

Epilogue

Believing in someone else strengthens both parties and your relationship.

55

Wage Peace in Your Relationships

Make your relationships peaceful ones. There is a great deal to say for working with others who are calm, rational, friendly, and easy to be around. On the other hand, when relationships are stormy and full of argument and emotion, the relationship is much more difficult to maintain.

```
┌─────────────────────────┐
│       Assignment        │
│                         │
│   Ideas 77 through 151 can │
│  help you wage peace in a variety │
│  of circumstances.      │
└─────────────────────────┘
```

Peaceful relationships are often much more positive and easier to maintain. If you are in a peaceful relationship, it's comfortable and rewarding. You are much more likely to seek out people like this than those with whom you have stormy relationships.

> ### Epilogue
> *Which would you rather have: peace or war? In relationships, it's clearly peace.*

56

Be a Peacemaker Between Friends

Throughout your career, you will occasionally find yourself in a position of having two friends that disagree heatedly about an issue. When that happens, you may have to make peace to get things back on track.

If you have to, be the go-between because you have a good relationship with each person. Or, you might need to call a private mediation between the three of you. But be cautious, however, about appearing to take one side or the other. Your goal is to facilitate, helping them hear and understand each other.

Just remember to remain neutral.

> **Assignment**
>
> Think back to a time when a friend helped you and another to hear and understand each other.

> **Epilogue**
>
> When necessary, help friends make peace with one another.

57

Respect Different Personality Types

Each person has his or her own personality type, which affects how he or she works, how he or she lives, and how he or she interacts with others—these personality types can be very different from each other. That's one of the things that makes people unique and interesting.

> **Assignment**
>
> Recognize the differing personality types around you, and find ways to understand and work with them.

It's important to recognize that not everyone operates the way you do. Type-A personalities may show up at work two hours early and stay two hours late, and then take work home with them. In contrast, a Type-C personality may do what she is assigned, arrive and leave on time, and likely not take work home.

These different types are all valid, and influenced by a combination of genetics and environment. So don't judge people based on their personality types. Instead, respect the traits of their type. They will not change for you, believe me!

Epilogue

People are different. Live with it.

58

Understand Different Styles

For years, social scientists have studied and classified different personal styles to help the military and corporations encourage better working relationships.

Assignment

Take a look at the four personality types. Which best describes you?

Personal styles are not to be confused with personality types. A Type-A personality could have a combination of two—and occasionally more—personal styles that make up his own individual approach to people.

So what are these personality styles? Well, there are several "systems" consultants and scientists have developed, but they almost all fall into the following four categories: the Analyzer, the Supporter, the Director, and the Creator.

In brief, the Analyzer is the thinker. She likes to investigate situations in detail, and prefers precision. The Supporter is, as you can imagine, sensitive and caring, tending to be sociable and co-operative with coworkers. The Director, on the other hand, is disciplined, results-oriented, and a practical problem-solver (think of Spock on *Star Trek*). And finally we have the Creator style; he is the free spirit in the group, both imaginative and innovative.

Seen them around the office? We bet!

Of course, these style labels are general in nature. Despite there being four definitive styles, most individuals combine two styles to develop their own unique approach to interacting with people. However, one style is usually dominant, and if you can identify it in someone, you can apply the Platinum Rule effectively—and figure out how best to interact with someone who leans toward a particular style.

Epilogue
When you understand someone's dominant personal style, you can better apply the Platinum Rule.

59

Recognize That Styles Differ From Opinions

Styles are not opinions. Styles are ways of behaving, ways of looking at and interacting with the world. People in each style category will still have opinions, but will base those opinions on varying information and approaches, and will likely come to different conclusions.

Regardless of personal style, a person's opinions are usually based on her principles and values, and can differ greatly from others in the same personal style category. For example, Analyzers will likely form their opinions primarily through facts. Supporters, by contrast, might weigh emotions and relationships. But they could share similar opinions on a particular issue or topic.

> **Assignment**
> Remember not to stereotype people's opinions based on their styles. Someone's personal style does not reflect his opinion, just his method for arriving at it.

The point is that, even if two people have the same personal style and may form opinions by a similar process, the opinions they arrive at could be worlds apart.

> **Epilogue**
> *Don't assume someone who has a similar personal style as you shares your opinions on issues and situations. Knowing personal styles is not a shortcut to listening to and understanding others.*

60

Know Your Own Style

So what is your style? It's nice to know others' personal styles, but it's also important to know your own—and how it is similar to or different from others with whom you interact regularly.

Are you predominately the Analyzer? Maybe the Supporter, or the Director? Or maybe you get to have all the fun as the Creator?

Does knowing this about yourself help you see why you might mesh or clash with some coworkers? Does it help you see that it's not that you're right and your coworker is wrong—or vice versa?

> ### Assignment
>
> To learn more about integrating your style with other personal styles, see Idea 61.

Can you also see why the Platinum Rule is just as important as the Golden Rule when developing relationships? Think about it. If you're a Creator, and a Director is trying to relate to you, maybe she is following the Golden Rule (she's treating you in a way that meshes with *her* style). But you're a Creator, right? So, treating you as she wants to be treated probably doesn't work for you. Instead she would need to apply the Platinum Rule. And you would need to do the same for her if you're truly going to have a solid relationship.

> ### Epilogue
> *Know thyself, and you will begin to know others.*

61

Stretch Beyond Your Style

To truly apply the Platinum Rule, you will have to stretch beyond your own style and try on another when interacting with others.

For example, if you are an Analyzer and you're working with a Supporter, then you will need think beyond the logical side of something and investi-

> **Assignment**
>
> Try elements from different styles to stretch yourself.

gate the emotions that drive the situation; numbers and statistics may not get you there. You may need to step out of your own personal comfort style and get into the head of your Supporter colleague—who works and comes to decisions based on how people feel.

Again, correctly applying the Platinum Rule requires you to stretch into another style, and truly try to understand how your colleague arrives at conclusions as he does. Then you can better determine what he needs, and you can use that approach to build emotional equity with him.

> ### Epilogue
> *Learning through experience is the best way to gain insight into the elements of personal styles.*

62

Embrace Different Styles

"Differing styles" does not have to equate to "conflicting styles." In fact, you should perceive them as complementary. Each person, with her own unique version of each style, brings a different approach and perspective to every action, event, or interaction.

There is great strength in this variety, if you recognize it.

> ### Assignment
>
> Value the different styles. Think about which styles apply to different people you know to help you understand them better.

Value people's differences and understand how strong work communities are built through this diversity. For example, the Creator brings innovation to the equation. The Director brings a focus on the practical. The Analyzer brings accuracy and an orderly, systematic approach to process. The Supporter is the people person, who brings emotion and harmony to the process.

With these varying styles, and their talents, you can look at an issue from four angles, instead of just one or two. Talk about seeing all sides!

> ### Epilogue
> *All styles are all valuable. Embrace them.*

63

Determine if You Are Shy

You enter a room or a situation with which you are unfamiliar. You don't know anyone. You've never been here before. Suddenly, your heart starts to beat rapidly and you break out in a sweat. You want to run. You want out of this situation.

80

If you have ever experi-
enced something similar to
this, you are probably shy. It's
the desire for withdrawal when
we face unfamiliar situations,
most often experienced in so-

cial settings. Many of us have experienced this, some more than
others. It can be a real barrier to building relationships if you can't
meet and get to know others.

Not you? Well, did you know that researchers estimate that as
much as 50 percent of the population of the United States is shy?
And that percentage is increasing.

If you are shy, then you need to work on overcoming shyness.
You need to be able to meet people and develop relationships with
them. If your shyness is getting in the way, you need to combat
that.

Epilogue

Shyness is a barrier to relationship-building.

64

Overcome Shyness

Some very famous and successful people were shy at one time,
and overcame it. Barbara Walters, Johnny Carson, Henry Fonda,
and Gloria Estefan were all considered shy at one time in their
lives. Obviously, they overcame the issue, and so can you.

81

Here are some tips for overcoming shyness:

* Work on your listening and communications skills.
* Learn more about reading nonverbal communication, such as body language and facial expressions.

> **Assignment**
>
> For more help with overcoming shyness, visit *www.overcoming-shyness.com*.

* Let others take the lead in conversations, then jump in after the discussion has begun.
* Observe others in environments that elicit shyness in you.
* Learn to smile. It's an ice-breaker.
* Learn to ask questions. That starts conversations.

These are just a few ideas. Shyness is a major barrier to developing relationships. Get more help with the following assignment.

> **Epilogue**
>
> *You can overcome being shy!*

65

Overcome Feeling Inferior

Feeling inferior to others is a matter of having low self-esteem. When you feel inferior to others, you believe that everyone else is better than you, either professionally or personally.

If you feel inferior to others, you need to do something about it. Just taking action can be empowering. You do need to take action,

Assignment

If you have this problem, take action. You might need to start with Idea 105.

because feeling inferior will be a barrier to creating meaningful relationships with others. And low self-esteem is often caused by real-world experiences—experiences that have somehow suggested that you don't measure up. Yet you can turn this situation around.

First, recognize that this feeling is almost always unfounded. Yes, you may well have had some bad experiences in which your ideas and actions did not achieve the desired result—we all experience that. But it's very likely you're just forgetting your successes, too focused on one situation or set of circumstances. Low self-esteem can leave us with a distorted view of reality, and that can be difficult to see around.

If you do need to make improvements, then make them. Failures are almost always caused by a series of factors. Find out what yours are. Do you need more training? Do you need a mentor? Do you need more experience? If so, take care of it.

Finally, remember that you do have strengths. Identify them and build on them. Use them as often as you can, and you will be rewarded with successes. And those successes will, in time, help combat the feeling of inferiority.

Recognize that no one is truly inferior to others. Inferiority is a barrier to creating positive relationships. Overcome that inferiority.

Epilogue

Eleanor Roosevelt once said, "No one can make you feel inferior without your consent."

66

Overcome Feeling Intimidated

Intimidation is similar to feeling inferior. The difference is that usually someone else has done something that has *made* us feel fearful or emotionally overwhelmed. But overcoming intimidation is essentially the same as overcoming feelings of inferiority.

> ### Assignment
>
> Overcome intimidation with the steps identified. You might want to start with Idea 105 first.

If you are feeling intimidated by someone, then you need to look at your relationship with that person. Is he the boss? Is she the office bully, domineering and reactive? If so, it's easy to see why you feel intimidated. And if your own emotional bank account is running on low or empty, you might need to replenish it (ideas 103 through 113) before you tackle this matter.

But if the intimidating feelings you're experiencing are founded on real threats or coercion, then you need to address the problem—by going to your human resources department, or even hiring legal counsel. Recognize that in these cases you are unlikely to be able to establish a positive relationship with this person.

Epilogue
You can beat intimidation if you are the problem. So do it.

67

Don't Be Too Talkative

Do you talk a lot—to the point of it being almost a social handicap?

There are many reasons for this, and being too talkative might integrate with

> ### *Assignment*
>
> If you talk too much, people will either avoid you or directly tell you so. Examine your situation and relationships to determine if you talk too much.

a dominant or opinionated approach. But usually it stems from fear and low self-esteem.

If you know this is you, you need to get your Chatty Cathy interactions under control. Being too talkative actually undermines your personal power and influence with others.

First, if you talk too much, people can't get their opinions and ideas into the conversation. People shy away from conversations with talkative people because they can't participate fully in the conversation. Secondly, talkative folks tend to eat up people's time. They know if they stop by your office to say good morning, it could take half an hour to get away again.

Although being social is a good thing, being overly talkative is a detriment to your relationships.

Epilogue

Being too talkative undermines your personal power and influence with others.

68

Listen, Don't Talk

The cure for being overly talkative is simple: listen.

Yep, just learn to listen more, and do it well. Social scientists tell us that effective communication between people needs to be equitable for relationships

Assignment

Skip ahead to Idea 85. If you think your talkative nature is more than just a bad habit, read ideas 103 through 113 first.

to take root. That means that we need to spend at least as much time listening as we do talking—and some cultures believe you should listen twice as much as you talk.

But if you find that your talkative nature is more than just an oversight or a habit gone awry, and it's based on feelings of insecurity or low confidence, then you need to fill your own emotional bank account first.

> ### Epilogue
> *Listening is the true cure for a talkative handicap.*

69

Get Out of Your Own Way

Think back to Idea 41. Remember those behaviors that can kill relationships? Well, those behaviors that become a pattern in

time can also become your
personal relationship ap-
proach. Three that are sure to
cause you problems are being
dominant, reactive, and aggressive or intimidating.

Consider these the three
deadliest approaches.

If you project any of these consistently with people, you could
be getting in your own way to success. Each of these approaches
can cause people to run the other way, or avoid you at every turn.
They can also cause you to live in an alternate reality—they can
lead you to believe things about yourself that just aren't true.

To get out of your own way and get on the path to success
with people, you have to fess up: Are you projecting one of the
three deadliest approaches?

Epilogue

*If you project any of the three deadliest approaches, you
could be getting in your own way to success.*

70

Douse the Domineering

Calling all domineering divas! If you're one of those people
who just knows it all, has an opinion about everything, and has to
always be in control, then you've come to the right chapter.

Though there are a number of new habits you'll need to develop to adopt a more effective approach, listening is by far the most important. That's right! You have to practicing listening—and lots of it.

Assignment

Read Idea 85. Then read 77 through 99 for more techniques to make over a domineering style.

Domineering styles are really just displays of pent-up energy generated by low self-esteem and fear. This person rarely demonstrates listening, and instead talks to deflect all possible and imagined threats. And these feelings of self-doubt run like a never-ending tape through a domineering person's brain.

But by listening—truly listening—you break the focus on your own fears and self-doubts, and instead put the focus on someone else. And that also redirects your energy from talking to listening in order to learn what's in someone else's head.

Epilogue

To transform a domineering approach, you have to practice listening—and lots of it.

71

Don't Be Reactive

Reactive people make us all nervous. And, frankly, if you're reactive, you know it. Either you're the guy who is pretty even-keel until someone pushes your hot buttons, or you're the guy who is always on edge, interpreting everything as an opportunity to blow.

First know that your reactive nature is driven by fear and self-doubt—particularly low self-confidence. However, you can start to get it back on track with three emergency techniques found in ideas 128, 131,

Assignment

Read ideas 128, 131, and 141. Then read 77 through 151. You need them all to truly transform your style to one that is much more effective.

and 141. These three must be used in combination, by (1) keeping your thoughts in check (Idea 128), (2) keeping your tongue in check (Idea 131), and (3) learning to ask questions to understand (Idea 141). This last step helps you keep egg off your face—something reactive folks tend to wear a lot.

Epilogue

You can nip a reactive outburst in the bud by holding your thoughts and tongue in check—in that order—and by asking questions to learn more.

72

Tackle the Intimidator

If you must win at all costs at even the first sign of disagreement, will resort to making personal attacks, slinging mud, and calling people out in front of others, then you've stopped at the right place.

The first thing you need to know is that people are avoiding you. They fear you, so you're not getting honest answers, good information, or acceptance. And that makes you ineffective in the workplace and other parts of your life.

89

But we want to help. Similar to the two other deadly approaches, you're running on fear. We believe you can change. Change starts with knowing that your approach

> **Assignment**
> Read this book cover to cover, but start with ideas 94, 106, and 109. These are a good starting point in transforming the intimidator approach.

is not okay; it's the deadliest of all when it comes to relationships— period! In fact, you will have the most work to do, but could end up holding the silent title of Most Improved among your coworkers.

> **Epilogue**
> *Projecting an intimidator approach makes a person ineffective in the workplace, and in other parts of life.*

73

Strive for Live Interaction

Today there are so many ways to communicate with each other: mobile phones, text messaging, instant messaging, e-mail, voice mail, and so on. But the most effective communication is not through high-tech, but high-touch.

> **Assignment**
> Give some face time today, and go high-touch!

By that we mean direct, daily, live interaction. We're talking face time here! To build good working relationships, you have to get out from behind the computer, the texting keyboard, and the mobile phone, and get in front of people.

Technology is all about logic, but people are emotional creatures (Idea 77). They don't connect with a message on a screen. They connect with faces and voices, and they need the other 80 percent of communication—body language and tone—that goes beyond words to make that connection (see Idea 133).

Epilogue

The most effective way to communicate with people is through high-touch, not high-tech.

74

Practice Face-to-Face Communication

From managing day-to-day relationships to resolving conflict and solving problems, face-to-face communication

Assignment

Make it a point this week to have your most crucial conversations face to face.

is the granddaddy of them all.

For decades, communication experts have been studying the most effective forms of communication, and face-to-face wins out again and again. You just get more done when you meet face to face with people. For one thing, we're usually all a little nicer to each other face to face, and we're all a little more relaxed. That nurtures better communication, for day-to-day interactions and for those times when situations are tense (see Idea 114).

> ### Epilogue
> *There is no better form of communication than face-to-face conversation.*

75

At Least Make It Live

All right, we understand that it just isn't possible to hold *every* conversation with someone face to face. So, when you can't, at least make it live with a phone conversation.

> ### Assignment
> For those conversations you just can't have face to face, make them live with an actual phone conversation.

That doesn't mean a voice-mail message. The conversation has to be *live*. You have to submit yourself to a flow of give and take, in which tone and inflection complement the words you and the other person are sharing.

Hey, don't discount it! Tone and inflection provide a wealth of information about the health of a conversation. And you can't get those from a sterile e-mail or text message. In fact, read on to Idea 76 to learn why we recommend using e-mail sparingly in working with others.

> ### Epilogue
> *In a live conversation, you get tone and inflection, which provide a wealth of information about the health of a relationship.*

76

Beware of E-mail

E-mail. The younger generation swears by it—lives by it. And yet it is the most ineffective form of communication for building and maintaining relationships.

Take Michelle, for example. When her staff

> ### Assignment
> Adopt Michelle's policy: If it takes more than two e-mails to resolve a situation, or get clarity on it, then go have a face-to-face conversation.

and another division found themselves with strained relationships, Michelle noticed that the vast majority of communication between their two groups was done via e-mail. And e-mail left a lot to be interpreted from mere words on a screen; most often the tone of those words was *mis*interpreted, and misunderstandings and hurt feelings ensued.

So, Michelle established a policy with her staff: If it takes more than two e-mails to resolve a situation, then her staff must get up and walk down the hall to meet with the other division's employee, or have a live phone conversation. Months later now, the two divisions have a great relationship. They work more collaboratively, they laugh more together, and each division supports and encourages the other.

The point? E-mail is no substitute for good ol' fashioned high-touch communication.

> **Epilogue**
>
> *If e-mail is your mainstay of communication, you need to expand your horizons to include high-touch interaction.*

77

Remember That People Are Creatures of Emotion

Though you may like to believe that people act from a place of rationality and reason, it would be a mistake to approach them with that expectation.

Assignment

Keep reading. There is so much more to learn about developing solid and effective relationships with people.

In fact, you would be flat wrong. As the great Dale Carnegie once said, "When dealing with people, remember you are not dealing with creatures of logic, but creatures of emotion."

People make up their minds about others and situations at an emotional level, and they interact through their emotions. Some are more in control of their emotions than others, but all are working from an emotional level nonetheless.

You have to remember that at all times. Your words, body language, and actions all trip emotional triggers in people. And depending on what words you use, what body language you demonstrate, and what actions you take, you can trip triggers that work in your favor, or work against you.

The following ideas provide you with a range of techniques and insights that can help you trip the right triggers—with authenticity and integrity that allows you to respect yourself and demonstrate respect for others.

Epilogue

People are not creatures of logic, but creatures of emotion—first, foremost, and always.

78

Fill the Emotional Bank Account

In working with people, you have to build emotional equity. You have to do things with every interaction that puts money in their emotional bank accounts.

> **Assignment**
>
> Read on!

You have to make deposits continuously, and withdrawals very rarely. In fact, one withdrawal with someone you have yet to build rapport with can put you at a deficit with that person so deeply that it could take years and multiple interactions to replenish it.

When you understand that people are emotional creatures, and work to take their emotions and feelings into account first, you give yourself the best chance of making deposits—and avoiding withdrawals.

The following ideas give explicit instructions and techniques for making deposits into people's emotional bank accounts—and how to replenish them when you run into disagreements, conflict, and flat-out confrontation.

Epilogue

To be successful in dealing with people, you have to build emotional equity with them at every interaction.

79

Make Friends

When it comes to making friends, Ralph Waldo Emerson said it best: "The only way to have a friend is to be one." And being a friend starts

> ### Assignment
>
> When you discover a connection point with someone, acknowledge it. Drop the person an e-mail, make a phone call, or stop by her office.

very simply—by finding a connection with the people you meet, and acting on it.

Likely, some of your best friendships started up because someone found that the two of you had something in common, or the person appreciated or valued something about you or your work. In short, the person found a connection point with you, and let you know it.

Finding and acting on connection points is easy—opportunities are staring you in the face every day. Take the standard office meeting, for example. As you listen to those around the table, find points on which you can connect with them. Then follow up afterward with someone whose point of view you valued, or whom you admired for having the courage to speak up.

Once you've made this first connection, you'll likely find that the person will return the support and encouragement down the road. And as you add up and act on these connection points in time, you'll very likely reap the rewards of friendship.

Epilogue

Look for ways you can connect with the people around you, then take action to recognize that connection and build on it.

80

Develop Your Emotional Intelligence

It does seem as though technical skills should be what's rewarded, doesn't it? After all, it's your technical skills that make you valuable, right?

Actually, you need a combination of both, and if you're going to be weak in one, studies

Assignment

Take stock of your people skills. Where are your strengths and weaknesses? Leverage your strengths, and learn what you can do to improve your weak areas. It will be well worth your effort.

show you're better off to be strong on the people skills and weaker on the technical side.

Why is that? Again, people are emotional creatures, and they don't care how much you know until they know how much you care.

That's right, you could be a technical genius, but if your people skills are lacking, you will very likely find your career stagnate or plateau. So, though you want to keep your technical skills sharp, you also want to sharpen your people skills to a fine point.

In short, you want to invest just as much, if not more time and energy in building up credits in your coworkers' emotional bank accounts. They will respect and remember the emotional equity you build with them long after the value of your technical skill has become yesterday's news.

Epilogue
You could be a technical genius, but, if your people skills are lacking, you will likely find your career stagnate or plateau.

81

Remember Names

Nothing shows basic respect for people more than remembering their names. Admit it—you like it when someone remembers your name after a first meeting. We all do. It makes us feel valued and respected.

Now remember a time when someone did not remember your name. Likely it felt awkward, and you probably looked on the person with a bit of suspicion or possibly even dislike. But when someone demonstrates he has made the effort to remember your name, an instant connection is formed. In fact, it's a first step in developing trust with others.

Remembering people's names is such a small thing, but has such a big impact on budding relationships. With one word, we communicate that we value someone else as a human being.

Assignment

Remember one key characteristic about the various people you meet, and assign their names to that picture in your mind.

Epilogue

By remembering someone's name, you extend the hand of respect and lay the foundation for friendship.

82

Look 'Em in the Eye

Okay, this is not a game of optical chicken, to see who blinks first. Looking someone in the eye is again one of those basic, yet often overlooked and underestimated ways to connect with people. Similar to remembering someone's name, looking someone in the eye is one of those subtle yet very powerful acts of respect.

Assignment

Focus your energy on making genuine eye contact, the kind that comes only from truly being engaged in the conversation, absorbing information, and using it to find connection points with the other person.

Forget all the superficial techniques you've learned about how to look at someone just above the brow line to show you're giving that person your attention. That's not authentic; that's BS. And people will know it.

Focusing on all the superficial techniques of listening, acknowledging, and providing feigned eye contact is often a distraction from doing what we really need to be doing—which is living in the moment with that one person, in that one conversation.

Looking someone in the eye comes naturally when you're listening and engaged in the conversation. If you do this, you'll be much more productive in building relationships and winning people's trust. And you'll earn their respect.

Epilogue
Looking someone in the eye demonstrates your respect for others and confidence in yourself.

83

Give Your Undivided Attention

Most of us today give subdivided attention, instead of undivided attention. The art of multitasking is to blame. We're busy checking the "crackberry" while a coworker is talking, or we're responding to e-mail or doing some other act of unintentional disregard.

As a result, we don't invest the time it really takes to build good relationships with people. So how do you cope with all the distracting demands that eat away at your attention span?

Simple: *stop!*

That means stop checking e-mail while talking to people on the telephone. Stop checking your BlackBerry while someone else is talking to you. Stop calling out to others while you're talking to a coworker in the hallway.

Giving subdivided attention is the result of a bad habit

> ### Assignment
> Observe your own behavior for a day, and make a list of your actions that say "I'm tuned out." Then think of ways you can stop doing them, and instead give people your undivided attention.

left unchecked. Put your PDA away during the meeting; you're there to *participate* in the meeting. Schedule time with a coworker who needs to talk, or tell her you'll stop in to see her later in the day. These are the techniques that say, "Hey, what you have to say is important, and I want to give it my undivided attention."

> ### Epilogue
> *Giving undivided attention is a forgotten art of relationship-building. Resurrect it, and your relationships will be stronger and last longer.*

84

Be "Present"

It's been said that 80 percent of success in life is just showing up. This is true, but if you're going to show up, shouldn't you do it mind and spirits too?

Being "present" is the best gift you can give those around you. It does take more interaction energy, but it also generates energy as well.

Ever been in a meeting when all were present? People were sharing ideas with enthusiasm, playing off one another's humor, laughing, making action plans, and so on. Think about how you felt when you left that meeting.

Did you feel lighter, more connected, good about the people, and energized to get moving with the mission?

There is a kind of magic that comes from people being present, and it's an infectious feeling. Work on being that kind of person, someone who is present, someone who lives in the moment of the situation, and finds the positive and possible in it.

This type of behavior attracts others to you, for your thoughts, your opinions, your advice, and your company.

Epilogue

If you're going to show up, be "present"—in body, mind, and spirit.

85

Practice Good Listening

The Japanese have a simple but insightful proverb that's worth posting somewhere near your desk. It goes like this: "Those who talk, sow; those who listen, reap."

The most important element of good listening is simple: You have to want to understand the other person's point of view. Listening is not about agreeing, or defending. It's not about how often you nod your head in the conversation, how many times you recap

Assignment

Look for at least three opportunities daily to listen to someone else, to understand what she thinks, fears, desires, and so on. Don't judge, argue, or defend your point of view; just listen—and learn.

what the person said, or how many affirmations you give to the other person. Those are techniques to help you become a better listener, but they are not listening in themselves.

The fundamental purpose of listening is to gather information about the other person, to understand where he's coming from, how she views a situation, or what he values. If you sit quietly and let others do the talking, you can have an excellent opportunity to learn, to gather information. And that can be very powerful—in several ways.

Most importantly, people are attracted to good listeners. Why? Because we all want to be heard—it's a common human desire. Good listeners give people that opportunity. And secondly, listening allows you to learn people's likes, dislikes, concerns, joys, and so on. By knowing more about people, you become much more effective in working with them.

Epilogue
Those who talk, sow; those who listen, reap.

86

Connect With People Through Questions

Being heard is a natural desire for all human beings. And so is sharing information about ourselves. Though we may not want to share *every* aspect of our lives, we do like for people to open the door and let us show them who we are.

Asking questions of others opens that door. When we ask others what they think

about a situation, a viewpoint, or about themselves or their work, we send the message that who they are is important.

As long as the questions are not prying, too personal, aggressive, or judgmental, most people will open up about themselves. And, when you pair that opportunity with your good listening skills, you have the chance to make a connection. In short, you get to know people better, and that gives you insight into how they tick—what makes them feel they way the do, what makes them act the way they do.

And when we know the people with whom we work better, we work better together.

> **Epilogue**
> Asking questions opens the doors for others to share who they are with you.

87

Be Careful With Your Opinions

Likely you've heard the old saying about opinions. It's not appropriate to repeat it in this book, but most people will agree the adage is true: Everyone has one.

And sometimes it's best to keep ours to ourselves—particularly our personal opinions. Think about it. You've met opinionated people, and aren't they annoying? Flaunting their personal opinions openly as if

> **Assignment**
> Throughout the next week, observe those around you who freely give their personal opinions. Note how you feel about them, how your coworkers and management respond to them, and how effective they are in working with others.

their view is *the correct view*? And these people usually have an opinion about everything and everyone.

Don't be one of these people. And if you are one of these people, keep reading.

Withholding your personal opinions can be a challenge, especially if someone's views differ at the deepest level from your own. In cases such as these, it might be best to politely avoid the conversation or change the subject altogether—such as with politics and religion. These, as you know, are topics that strike at people's most core values. And they are usually emotionally charged.

So how do you hold a give-and-take conversation in which you're fully engaged to a make a connection—all without giving your opinion? Ask questions, then listen. Ask questions, then listen. And when and where you can agree, say so.

However, in the course of your daily work, you'll need to give your professional opinion. When doing so, be sure to shape your response so that your opinion doesn't come off as the *only* view—because it never is. People who know you and trust you, the people you've made connections with, will see the value in your opinion and support its merit.

Remember: Giving your personal opinion is just a way to get attention. There are 151 smarter ideas in this book for getting the right kind of attention—the kind that wins you friends and influences people.

Epilogue
Everyone has an opinion, and sometimes it's best to keep ours to ourselves.

88

Withhold Judgment

A judgment goes further than just agreeing or disagreeing with someone's viewpoint. Instead, a judgment predetermines how effective you'll be in working with someone. In short, when you pass judgment on someone, you adjust your behavior to align with your opinion about him or something associated with him.

And is that really fair? We don't like it when someone judges us—particularly when that person doesn't really get to know us. At some point, we have all been stung by the feeling of being judged by someone who doesn't have all the facts, or by someone who suffers from ethnic, gender, or lifestyle prejudice, or professional jealousy.

> ### *Assignment*
> Make a list of the people in your office with whom you have difficulty. What judgments have you made about them? Are those judgments holding you back from developing a more effective working relationship?

Judging others gives us some misguided permission to dislike someone—or worse—and to act upon it.

So, how do you withhold judgment of others? Get to know them. Invite a conversation, ask them questions, find out what drives them, what they want to accomplish with a project, their career, their lives, and so on. You may find you have more in common than you had imagined.

> ### Epilogue
> *Making judgments of others limits how effective you will be in working with them.*

89

See Both Sides

There are indeed two sides—or more—to every issue or argument. And people will trust and respect you if you show them you can see the different dimensions of a situation, and not just the one you prefer.

By actively seeing both sides, you show people you are fair, thoughtful, and respectful—all traits that make up the people we usually admire the most.

It's easy to align ourselves to the familiar, or to argue against the unfamiliar. But the person who can stretch beyond what she knows or feels comfortable with, and

Assignment

Consider a coworker or family member with whom you are at odds. Think about why you are at odds, and then think about the other person's viewpoint. Think of some questions that can help you get better insight into that person's approach to the situation. Next, plan an opportunity to politely ask your questions, also with your best intentions in play.

seek to understand a different view or experience, is truly the gifted among us.

In fact, people who can see both sides of an issue are usually viewed as more credible. They're open-minded—open to change, and open to having their minds changed—and people naturally gravitate to them, or seek them out.

When we open ourselves up and see differences in views, approaches, and practices, we open ourselves up to a range of possibilities, and a variety of solutions. And we gain a golden opportunity to learn about those around us.

Epilogue

Seeing both or multiple sides of an issue or situation shows you are a fair, interested person bent on seeking the middle ground.

90

Edify, Edify, Edify

The word *edify* comes originally from the Latin, meaning "to build." And when others aren't around but become a topic of discussion, that's exactly what you should do: build them up in their absence. Any time you speak about a coworker, boss, or col-

> ### Assignment
>
> Write down three positive things you can say about all of your coworkers. The next time you're tempted to run any of them down, let the positive words you've prepared come out of your mouth instead.

league, always speak positively about her. Never tear someone down, gossip about, or demean someone who is not around to defend himself.

It's bad manners and poor form to run others down. And though most will never say it to your face, people listening to you run someone else down are secretly wondering if you do the same to them when they're not around.

Sometimes Mom's adage is true: If you don't have anything nice to say, then don't say anything at all.

But if you must say something, find honestly positive things to say, such as: "I know John can be direct, but he's very intelligent," or "Lisa has had a rough year, but she's bringing a lot of value to our team."

When people hear you edify others who are absent, they trust you will do the same for them when they are not around.

Prove them right!

109

> ### Epilogue
> Remember: When you sling mud, you always get some on yourself.

91

Give Honesty With an Equal Dose of Compassion

It's been said that honesty without compassion is cruelty.

Yes, it's true that we do prefer people who are straight up with us. We all want to know where we stand. But ever met someone who prides herself on brutal honesty? Someone who feels at ease saying whatever comes to mind—all in the name of "just being honest"?

> ### Assignment
> Think of a situation in which you feel you must be honest with someone, then consider how you would like someone to share the same information with you. If you're really honest with yourself on this second step, you'll find a compassionate way to be honest with someone else.

There is a wide difference between "telling it like it is" and compassionate honesty. Usually people who are brutally honest lack something crucial in developing relationships. It's called tact. And tact stems from a sense of compassion.

But just what exactly is compassion? In short, it's a measure of sensitivity. It's knowing that, often, people are unaware that their behavior or actions are rubbing us the wrong way. It's understanding that people come from different walks of life, and their behaviors are a result of their culture—domestic, foreign, or family. And that difference doesn't equate to inferiority.

So when you find you need to "tell it like it is," tell it with compassion. Let the person know you have his best interests at heart, and you want good things for him. Share facts without judgment, and choose language that demonstrates you believe the best of this person.

When you mix honesty with compassion, you have the right ingredients for friendship and respect.

Epilogue

When you find you must tell it like it is, tell it with compassion.

92

Help Others Be Heard

Sometimes it falls to us to help others to be heard. Not everyone is assertive. Some people are shy, or feel intimidated in group settings. Be on the lookout for these folks. Too often they can be bulldozed by the aggressive or dominant personalities in the bunch. And they need help from more assertive coworkers such as yourself.

By helping others to be heard, you foster an environment of inclusion, an atmosphere such that all are welcome and valued.

When you see someone hanging back in a meeting or group discussion, purposefully ask for her viewpoint, or what she thinks about one of your ideas. Make a concerted effort to help her feel safe, and encourage her to participate.

It's particularly important to extend this effort to those new to the group, from another division, or from an outside organization. And it's especially critical when you have a mix of senior- and junior-level employees. Senior-level employees are used to elbowing their way through; that's how many got where they are—right or wrong. Junior-level employees who are not used to working with senior leadership may feel particularly intimidated.

> **Assignment**
>
> Scout the room the next time you are in an office meeting and identify those who have not had a chance to participate—and make an opportunity for them to be heard.

When you help these coworkers to be heard, you can set the stage for someone to shine. And *you* are sure to gain an admirer in the process.

> **Epilogue**
> *When you help others to be heard, you create an environment of inclusion in which others feel welcome and valued.*

93

Help Others Be Understood

It also falls to us sometimes to help others to be understood. There are lots of reasons for this. Sometimes people have difficulty articulating their ideas, or they are an outsider for some reason and need a champion.

In these cases, you have the opportunity to be a translator and a champion.

But you want to approach these opportunities with delicacy, and not dominance. Mishandling these situations could paint you as a know-it-all.

So how do you proceed without making a mess of it? Think facilitation. The next time you see a colleague's input being met with puzzled expressions from the group, summarize what you think the person is saying and

> ### Assignment
> Seek out opportunities to help others to be understood, whether that is to get their point across, to clear up a misunderstanding with the boss or a coworker, or to demonstrate their unique contribution to the group.

then ask if your summation is correct. It may require some give and take for a few minutes, but if you're patient and genuine about understanding, you will help your colleague get his point across.

This technique, if handled with sincerity and good intentions, is powerful. Your colleague will feel as though he has an advocate, and he will remember the gesture.

Voila! You've made a connection!

> ### Epilogue
> *When you help someone to be understood, you have an opportunity to be someone's champion.*

94

Allow People to Save Face

In Asian culture in general, it is considered better to be silent than to point out someone's error in front of others. This is a cardinal rule in a number of Eastern cultures. It's called saving face, and it's an act of respect.

In Western culture, we're often more interested in winning, more interested in being right, more interested in showing our expertise. We're more interested in these bragging rights than giving another some leeway to be wrong.

> ### *Assignment*
> Observe a colleague who does not know the rule of saving face. Watch how others respond to this person.

But those who have strong people skills often take a lesson from the Eastern cultures, and let their colleagues save face. When they hear ideas or statements of fact that are off the mark, they address those in private with the person—not out in the open for all to see and hear.

Think about it. You don't like to be told you are wrong in front of others either. Learning that we've been wrong in some way is never easy to hear, but being told in front of others is just adding insult to injury.

Just as your colleague will appreciate you for helping her to be heard or understood among others, she will also appreciate it when you let her save face among them as well.

Epilogue
Being told we're wrong is never easy—but being told in front of others is just adding insult to injury. Always allow others to save face.

95

Encourage

All people need encouragement. It is the fuel that keeps us going, that helps us pick ourselves up when we're feeling down,

```
┌ ━ ━ ━ ━ ━ ━ ━ ━ ━ ━ ━ ━ ━ ━ ━ ━ ━ ━ ┐
┃              Assignment               ┃
┃   Look for opportunities daily to encourage others. Listen
┃   to them, understand them, and then lift them up.
└ ━ ━ ━ ━ ━ ━ ━ ━ ━ ━ ━ ━ ━ ━ ━ ━ ━ ━ ┘
```

and allows us to keep moving forward. Encouragement is the balm that covers our hurts and gives us faith that "this too shall pass." And it is the fire that spurs us to greater heights and drives us to stretch ourselves farther than we ever thought we could travel.

You can be a source of encouragement for others. You can be the well people come to when they need a dose of inspiration, the mirror that helps them see their strengths when all they see is their weaknesses, the fire that fuels their dreams and launches them to new endeavors.

To offer encouragement is not to forgo reality, or be unrealistically optimistic. In fact, being overly optimistic will make others doubt you, thinking you lack objectivity. But to genuinely encourage others is to help them see what is and what can be. It is about taking the truth, mixing it with reason, and helping others to see it for themselves.

Epilogue

To genuinely encourage others is to help them see what is and what can be.

96

Encourage With Words and Perspective

When you are striving to encourage someone else, look to words and perspective to help you.

Sometimes encouraging words might be something as simple as "hang in there" when someone is having a bad day. Other times you might need to track down a quote from an inspiring source, such as a writer, philosopher, historical figure, or spiritual icon, and put it into an e-mail. And sometimes you might just need to write down what you value about that person and send it in a card to be read again and again.

Assignment

Check out Websites such as *www.inspirational-quotes.info* for convenient access to encouraging quotations from people throughout history. Share these whenever you see someone in need of a lift.

When listening to a colleague who needs a boost, look for opportunities to put her thoughts into a realistic perspective. Help her see where her words might be off the mark. For example, we often hear people make comments about themselves such as "I can't ever seem to get it right," or "the boss really hates me." Let these words be a red flag telling you to step in. Phrases such as these are overgeneralizations or exaggerations, and you need to check them with your own observations: "Mary, that's not true. You get it right a lot. You're just having an off day/week." Or, "Mary, the boss values you. He's just having a rough week. He's been a little cross with everyone the past few days."

Your words and perspectives can be a light for someone during a dark week. When you see the opportunity to illuminate his situation with encouraging words and perspectives, do it.

Epilogue

Your words, insights, and observations can help encourage others. Step up and use these tools to build emotional equity with someone today!

97

Pat Others on the Back

Sometimes encouraging someone is as simple as an attaboy, a pat on the back, a little recognition for a job well done.

And sometimes it falls to us to give it to others—coworkers and bosses alike. Yep, that's right: Even the boss needs a pat on the back occasionally. We often think the boss is recognized enough, but you would probably be surprised to find how little top executives recognize their management when they hit the mark.

Assignment

For your records only, keep a list throughout the week of coworkers' and the boss's good works. Then make it a habit to take the last hour of every Friday to send an "attaboy" e-mail of recognition to those on your list. Your note will be one of the first they will see when they start their day on Monday.

Of course, this often trickles down. Middle and frontline management lead by example, and if their boss isn't handing out pats on the back, they usually don't either. So it sometimes falls to the coworker—the one who works most closely with us, who sees our daily struggles and minute victories—to pat us on the back and let us know our efforts have not gone unnoticed.

Be that person every chance you get. Be on the lookout for good works, and give a pat on the back whenever you can. Of course, do it with sincerity. Remember, again: no sucking up! People can smell phoniness a mile away.

Epilogue
Be on the lookout for good works, and give a pat on the back every chance you get.

98

Be a Cheerleader

Being a cheerleader for someone is a big stretch. It takes a lot more than words and listening. Being a cheerleader takes energy and diligence. It takes commitment.

> **Assignment**
> Find someone to cheer on. But be selective. Being someone's cheerleader is a long-term and intense investment of energy and diligence.

And the reward you will gain is usually more long-term than short-term.

When you commit to being someone's cheerleader, you will gain someone's lifelong respect. Cheerleading for someone is more about driving them toward a goal; it can mean you have to pick her up out of the doldrums again and again. It could mean you have to keep dusting her off, and putting her back on track. It means that as long as you see that person earnestly striving for her goal, you never give up.

Being someone's cheerleader requires you to plant seeds of hope with that person regularly, sometimes day in and day out. Parents and successful leaders know this to be a fact. And being a cheerleader means you have to nurture people with attaboys, encouraging words, and insight. You will need to do it consistently throughout time.

118

And when that person achieves his goal, whether it's a promotion, a new job, earning a college degree, or crossing a lifelong personal bridge, that someone you cheered on will remember you. In fact, he will remember you years down the road, long after you have lost touch and your working relationship is a thing of the past. Your investment of energy and diligence *will* be remembered.

Epilogue

Being someone's cheerleader requires you to plant seeds of hope with that person regularly, sometimes day in and day out. But when you commit to being someone's cheerleader, you will gain someone's lifelong respect.

99

Help Others Achieve Their Goals

Goals are often the guidelines of our lives. They keep us focused, on the path to what we want the most. And we often need people to help us reach them.

In reaching our goals, we first have to define them. You can

Assignment

Look around the office for those who seem downtrodden and help them define and set their goals. Then help them when and where you can to achieve their goals.

do this for others, and encourage them to achieve them. Take Michael, for example. At age 50 he found himself downsized from a career that had never lived up to his expectations, his savings drained, and his spirit numb from a life of strife and stress. He moved with the weight of the world on him, his head hung low, his shoulders hunched. In short, he was the walking wounded.

But with the help of a caring coworker, Michael realized that his healing had to begin with reviving a lifelong goal he had long thought was dead: He wanted to finish his college degree. An articulate and intelligent person, he had made his way in the world for himself and his family for many years without it. But it always ate at him.

That same coworker encouraged Michael to go back to school, to do it for himself, alone, to prove to himself that he had no deficiencies. Within just a few weeks of starting back at college, Michael's demeanor began to change. He smiled and joked more, he walked straighter, and he looked people in the eye with confidence. Working toward his goal gave him a focus, a path to follow, and hope.

Goals do that for us. And when we help others achieve their goals, we help them realize a piece of their purpose.

> ### Epilogue
> *When we help others achieve their goals, we help them realize a piece of their purpose.*

100

Let Others Shine

If you find yourself always seeking the spotlight, ask yourself why. Is it because you want others to notice you, such as the boss, coworkers, or the CEO? Often we are turned off by those who earnestly seek the spotlight. And, ironically, we admire those who consistently point out the achievements and accomplishments of others. In short, we respect those who seek out ways to let *others* shine.

Take top quarterback Peyton Manning for example. Though he

> ## *Assignment*
>
> Make a list of opportunities in which you can recognize or recommend a coworker—then act on it.

is the best of the best in the National Football League, in interview after interview with the media he seeks out opportunities to compliment his fellow players, and to remark on their contributions to winning the game.

Letting someone shine can be as simple as giving someone the floor to present a new idea, pointing out someone's accomplishment in the staff meeting, or sending an e-mail to the whole team recognizing a coworker's help with a recent project.

You can let someone shine also by recommending them for a high-profile project, or nominating them for a company bonus or award.

Instead of investing your energy to get yourself in the spotlight, figure out ways each day to let someone else bask in the limelight. You might be surprised at the mutual admiration club you will create, and how often others will return the gesture.

Creating opportunities to let others shine will demonstrate that you are a team player. And being a team player will gain you more in the long run than striving to be noted as the team superstar.

Epilogue

When you make way for others to shine, you show you are a team player.

121

101

Look for Reasons to Celebrate

Life should be a celebration. It's a gift, after all. And given how much time we all spend on the job—and how hard we work—the office is a great place to create celebrations each day. So why not look for reasons to celebrate?

The reasons can be both professional and personal. For

> ### *Assignment*
>
> Get out the list again, and this time jot down events and accomplishments in the office you can celebrate with others—then start planning those celebrations.

example, did a coworker just buy her first house? Did someone pass a professional certification exam? Did a group just come through a tough project victoriously?

Celebrations can be acknowledged with a cup of coffee, a plate of cookies, or a full-blown celebratory dinner complete with cocktails. For example, if your coworker just purchased her first home, you could show your joy for her with a congratulatory box of donuts and a card. The point is not about creating an extravagant ceremony, but rather to create a moment for others to stop and smell the roses.

In short, celebrations give you an opportunity to let others shine, point out people's hard work, and let them know they matter. You will find your own spirits lifted when you take time to celebrate life's moments.

> ### Epilogue
> *The point of creating celebration is to make time to stop and smell the roses with others.*

102

Remember Birthdays, Anniversaries, and Such

Birthdays and anniversaries are ready-made opportunities to celebrate—and a great way to remind people that they matter to you. Acknowledging anniversaries and birthdays is also a way to let others know they are remembered, and you can turn it into a fun trip down memory lane.

> ### *Assignment*
> Set an alarm on your electronic calendar to remind you of people's birthdays and anniversaries. Then reach out to them on those special days.

For example, get the team together for a short celebration to remember someone's five-year office anniversary. Have everyone tell a funny story they remember from that person's first year in the office. Or organize one big birthday pitch-in lunch for all those celebrating birthdays in a given month.

Of course, a short e-mail wishing someone a happy anniversary or happy birthday is just as special to coworkers working halfway around the world, or just remotely from another location.

The point, again, is not how elaborate you can be, but rather to acknowledge people on special days. In short, birthdays and anniversaries are a way to connect with people.

Epilogue

Use birthdays and anniversaries as yet another reason to connect with people throughout the year, and to celebrate knowing them.

103

Fill Your Own Emotional Bank Account

To keep up with the continual task of building up others' emotional bank accounts, you have to make sure yours is filled as well. This is absolutely critical, because, if you're running on emotional empty, you will have nothing to give to others.

Assignment

Continue reading. The following ideas discuss ways to keep your own emotional bank account filled.

Taking care of your own emotional needs is highly important when you take on the challenge of practicing excellent people skills. And there are several ways you can do that. The first is to know what your needs are, how to feed them, and how to surround yourself with people who help you keep your emotional bank account filled.

You also need to know when you're approaching "people burnout," and what you need to do to cope with it. And when you deal with people enough over your career, you *will* experience people burnout to some degree. Like death and taxes, it's inevitable.

The trick is to be self-aware enough to know the signs, and to head it off before it escalates to a full-blown case of burnout. If you don't, you could undo a lot of great work in a very short time. And when you're starting from less than zero, it's hard to rebuild.

Epilogue

If you run on emotional empty yourself, you will have nothing to give to others' emotional bank accounts.

104

Feed Your Own Needs

Be careful of running on empty. Managing relationships with people takes energy, and, depending on where you get your energy, you could burn out on the "people thing" pretty quick.

Make sure you take care of the basics, such as getting three square meals a day, a good night's sleep as often as possible, and some alone time. If

Assignment

Take time to reflect on what recharges you, and take stock of when you know you're approaching burnout. Being aware of these two indicators can help you know when to stop, and when to push forward.

you're an introvert, as defined by the Myers-Briggs assessment, then you will need additional alone time because solitude is how you recharge your batteries. However, extroverts on the Myers-Briggs scale tend to need frequent interaction with people to rev up their energy levels.

The point here is to feed your individual needs. Know what you need to maintain balance in your own life. If you're out of balance, you will be off kilter in dealing with others. And when you get off kilter, conflict and confrontation with others usually are not far behind.

When you hit a wall, take a step backward and take care of yourself. Do not push yourself when you are running on empty. Stop and refuel, recharge, and take care of yourself.

Epilogue

Remember to stop and feed your own needs. Know what it takes to help you maintain balance in your own life.

105

Call on Your Support Group

When you start feeling yourself lose steam in dealing with your coworkers, call on your support group. You know who we mean: the friends who help you laugh at yourself and your situation, the friends who put things into perspective for you, or your personal cheerleading squad.

Assignment

When you feel as though you have hit a wall with the "people" part of your job, or life in general, call on your support group to help you sort it out. Reach out and let them do what they were put in your life to do—support you with friendship.

This could be a group of friends, your best friend, a close sibling, a parent, or a mentor. Striving to have good relationships with coworkers can be draining, and sometimes leaves us in doubt, or in need of an ear to bend for an hour or so.

Sometimes they can simply help you take your mind off a situation for a while. They can make you laugh, remember better times, and paint a more optimistic picture when people and situations bring you down.

Be ready for this very real possibility: Managing relationships with people will have its down moments, no matter how astutely you deal with others. People are people, and you cannot control them. You can only control yourself, your reactions, and your attitude. Your support group helps you do just that.

Epilogue
Remember that, when you deal with people, you can only control yourself. Your support group helps you keep all systems in check.

106

Keep Honest Company

Though we want friends who will listen to us without judging or criticizing, we also want them to be honest—and call us on our own bull when we need it. These are the friends who are comfortable enough to set us straight when we need it, but who also give us room to make our own choices and mistakes.

Assignment
Tell a friend this week that you appreciate his honesty, and value his willingness to set you straight when you need it.

This is the kind of company you want to keep. As you strive to improve how you interact with people, your honest friends will make the best sounding boards. They are the ones who will keep you from letting rationalization persuade you that a bad action is a good one. And they will tell you when you mess up.

Precisely because they are daring enough to call you out when you fumble, they are also the ones you can truly trust when they tell you have done something right.

In short, you want your support group to be made up of honest people, those who have your best interests at heart, and will steer you in the right direction when it looks as though you might be veering off course. These are the friends worth having.

Epilogue

An honest friend is one who will speak up and tell us what we need to hear.

107

Get Inspired

The people in our lives who see us as bigger and bolder than we see ourselves are the best friends to have. These are the people who inspire us—they tell us to believe, they show us *how* to believe, and they convince us *to* believe.

People who inspire us are like a well, filling us up with

Assignment

Plan lunch or coffee this week with a friend who inspires you and lifts you up. He or she can help you rise above the pettiness of the workplace and inspire you to be more than you already are.

courage and creativity. They give us direction, and they get us moving forward. And we all need them in our lives.

In working with people, particularly difficult personalities, day in and day out, you can lose sight of who you are—and where you're going. Managing your people skills is work, and it can be tiring work that can leave you feeling empty some days.

On those days when dealing with your coworkers, boss, or anyone else, who has torn you down, find time with a friend who inspires you. Let her remind you of who you are, from where you have come, and what you can be.

When you feel inspired, you can find your courage, your creativity, and your compassion—all the skills you need to be your best with people.

Epilogue

An inspiring friend reminds you of who you are, from where you've come, and what you can be.

108

Find Friends Who Edify You in Your Absence

You need friends and colleagues who have your back. Just as you should edify others (see Idea 90) in their absence, your friends should as well.

Assignment

Take stock of your closest office confidantes. Would they have the courage and inclination to defend and edify you in your absence?

These are the kinds of people who will defend you if you're spoken of out of school in your absence. These are the people who will keep your confidences, and will speak to your positive attributes and defend your honor when you're not around.

Nothing is more deflating and depleting than learning a co-worker has dogged you out of earshot, or failed to defend you when maligned by another colleague. Those in your support group who cannot do this should be removed from the list—and added to another.

In short, those who are truly your friends should deflect mud when it's being slung in your direction, and you should do the same for them.

Epilogue

Just as you want to edify others when they are not present, you owe it to yourself to associate with others who will do the same for you, in your absence.

109

Find a Class Act to Follow

By now, you have probably gotten the point multiple times that practicing effective people skills is hard work. It takes diligence and commitment, and role models.

By "role model" we mean a class act, someone who models what you want to practice. In this case, you will want to seek out role models who already demonstrate good people skills.

When you spend time with role models, you get to see examples of effective people skills in action. For example, many business and sports leaders admire John Wooden, the famed basketball coach who is considered an all-around class act. Wooden is noted as a polished individual who approaches people with compassion, honesty, and encouragement. And because of that, he is noted in history as of the most effective and revered coaches in sports.

Being exposed frequently to a class act gives you a pattern to follow; it gives you living examples to follow. When you are feeling unsure in a situation, you can pull from memory how one of your role models handled a similar challenge, and imitate him.

> ## Assignment
>
> Identify those in your circle who demonstrate solid people skills, and find ways to spend time with them. Watch them, listen to them, learn how they think, and then imitate their polished skills every chance you get.

Yes, we're telling you to "fake it to make it" on occasion. But with practice and repeated exposure to a class act, you'll see yourself becoming more like the company you keep.

> ### Epilogue
> *With repeated exposure to a class act, you'll find yourself becoming like the company you keep.*

110

Take a "People Break"

Life in general today can wear you down. But when you add in the people factor, and all the energy it takes to deal with them effectively, you can really find yourself feeling drained.

Be alert to when your batteries are running low, and your tolerance levels with people are approaching the bottom. These are times when you could say or do something you will later regret, and commit a career-limiting move.

When you start feeling that you are tapped out with people, take a people break. Just go off

> ## Assignment
>
> Think back to times when you reached your people limit for the day. What happened when you pushed yourself beyond that limit? Did you have a spat with a coworker or say something you regret?

to yourself for a few minutes, or a few hours if possible. Change your scenery; get out of the office for a quick walk.

Of course, sometimes getting away from the office just isn't possible. If you know you're at the end of your rope and it is only 10:30 a.m. and your calendar is taunting you with four more meetings to come, take an interaction break. That means limiting how much interaction you engage in with others for the remainder of the day. This might be a good time to practice your listening skills, rather than your speaking skills. You can still be polite; you just don't have to indulge in in-depth conversations.

The point is to back off when you're feeling as though you've reached your people limit for the day. Making the effort to dial down your interaction levels at these times can be critical to your success—both professionally and personally.

Epilogue

When you start feeling tapped out, take a people break.

132

111

Sharpen the Saw by Sharpening Your Mind

Read, read, read! Reading helps to keep your mind sharp. Just as what you put in your mouth affects your body's health, what you put into your mind also affects how you think. So as you're working to improve how you relate to people, read up on topics such as communicating more clearly, human psychology, or how to manage conflict.

> **Assignment**
>
> Get on the Web and check out an online bookstore, or your local library, to get a list of books about people and people skills. Then set a goal to read one book a month for the next year. If you apply what you learn, you will find yourself handling people like an expert.

Take time out every now and again to add to what you already know, or explore an area about people about whom you would like to learn more. For example, if you're a Baby Boomer working with GenXers or Millenials, you might want to read up on intergenerational relationships in the workplace. Adding more to your mental repertoire through reading will not only help you expand your understanding, but it will also expand your vocabulary and give you a broader range of words to choose from in relating to others.

Don't make it a grueling assignment; just select something in which you're interested and head to the local bookstore or library. And, of course, the Internet is filled with quick reads and articles that can be helpful as well.

In short, sharpening your mind is a great way to sharpen your people skills.

Epilogue
Take time out to add to what you already know about dealing with people. Read, read, read!

112

Get Away From Your Desk for Lunch

Get out for lunch, either alone or with a friend. The lunch hour is a great time to take a people break, to refuel, refresh, and prepare to take on the second half of the day.

Step out in the sunshine, take a walk through the park, or tuck away in a coffee shop and read a

Assignment

If you're a desktop luncher, make it a point to get out at least once this week, then twice next week, and so forth. You will be surprised how much better you will feel after a leisurely lunch away from your desk.

book. If you don't like eating alone in a public place, then bring your lunch and find a quiet spot in the office, such as a conference room. Take along the iPod and listen to your favorite tunes while you munch on your favorite sandwich.

Or bring a friend along and play a game of "That's Wild." To play, you simply share the most bizarre thing you've heard all week on the news, or the strangest thing to happen to you that day or week. There are only two rules: The first is, whatever you share has to be funny or comically strange. The second is, you cannot talk office politics or gossip.

The point is that, when lunchtime rolls around, you need to get up, get moving, get some chow, and get a change of scenery and perspective. You'll come back feeling refreshed and ready to tackle the rest of the day.

Epilogue

When lunchtime rolls around, get up, get moving, and get out.

113

Attend Social Events

Get out your social calendar and start making plans. In fact, you should plan one social outing a week—or more.

Applying your people skills all day at the office can be draining, so recharge your bat-

> **Assignment**
>
> Get out your calendar and plan one social event a week. Go! Do it now!

teries with some time out with your girlfriends, guy friends, or significant other. Take in a game, go to a concert, head for the local pub, or attend a church event. Which social activities you attend are completely up to you, but you need them mixed into your week to keep you balanced. And you need balance to keep your people skills on track.

Social events give you a chance to let your hair down around people you know or who have similar interests. They let you express

135

yourself, and they give you an opportunity to make new friends and increase your circle of connections.

Think of your weekly social event as the light at the end of the tunnel, a bright spot in the week to which you can look forward when the workplace drags you down.

Epilogue

Social events can be a light at the end of the tunnel for a tough work week. Add them to your weekly routine.

114

Handle Conflict With Confidence

Up to now we've covered, for the most part, how to get along with others. But what about those times when disagreement hinders or threatens to derail our excellent-people-skills mission?

Assignment

Keep reading. There is much more for you to learn and put into practice.

We're glad you asked, because that means you're smart. This question shows that you have realistic expectations of your relationships with people. Conflict is a natural part of life, and you cannot work with people 52 weeks out of the year without having occasional disagreements, conflicts, and sometimes confrontations.

But when these are handled correctly, they don't have to derail your efforts. In fact, they can make your relationships with people stronger, and more honest.

Managing your interpersonal skills through conflict can actually make you a stronger communicator, able to handle more than just the convenient and easy situations. After all, someone who can face conflict and disagreement productively is a much more effective employee than someone who just avoids it.

So, yes, conflict will arise. And with the following tips, techniques, and insights, you will be able to handle them like a pro.

Epilogue

Conflicts, handled appropriately, can actually lead to stronger, more honest relationships.

115

Can't We All Just Get Along?

Can't we all just get along? Unfortunately, no. Not always.

If you expect people to always get along, you will be disappointed. Some people will never get along because they do not want to put

Assignment

When you encounter someone who refuses to extend the hand of respect, practice your listening skills. Speak less in these situations, maintain professional courtesy, and limit your interaction with this person.

in the work necessary. And, as you have learned thus far in this book, getting along with others in a way that creates a win-win daily takes a lot of work.

Some people just don't want to make that effort. And there are people who don't want to play by the same rules. They don't think they have to be considerate, respectful, fair, compassionate, and so on. Others may believe themselves to be superior to others for some reason, either due to position, authority, social status, wealth, politics, or religious beliefs.

You are not one of these people, of course. But you will encounter others who are. It is an unfortunate fact of life. And we all have to contend with these folks at some point or other—in some work environments, you may have to contend with them every day.

Accepting the fact that people will just not be inclined to get along with you or others is not to say that you should be on the lookout for these folks. The point is to accept that we cannot always get along with some people.

So, what do to? When you encounter someone who repeatedly shows you she is not willing to do her part to get along with you, be polite, be respectful, but limit your interaction with this person. If you have made a sincere effort to make a connection with her and she does not return the effort, then the problem becomes hers.

As long as you take the high road, you have nothing to feel bad about. Just continue to be yourself and get on with your day.

Epilogue

Manage your own expectations; people will not always get along. It's a fact of life with which we all have to contend.

116

365 Opportunities for Conflict— 366 in a Leap Year

Every day and every conversation is a potential for conflict. Though you may enter each with good intentions, you cannot control others' responses or reactions. So as with getting along with others (Idea 114), you also need to temper your expectations when it comes to conflict.

With 365 days in a year, and 366 in a leap year, there

Assignment

Read on. The following ideas describe strategies for how to manage conflict when you experience it.

is much opportunity for you to experience disagreements or confrontations with others. The foolish person seeks to avoid them altogether. The smart person has a strategy ready for when they arise, because arise they will.

There are several strategies for diffusing conflict and turning it into something productive, but which to use depends on the situation. Some conflict comes from misunderstandings, or miscommunications. Some comes from a lack of information or a lack of communication. And some comes from the people described in Idea 114—they just feel they have no responsibility to get along with others.

Each of these requires a different strategy, and most can be diffused and converted into rapport over time. You just need to know which strategy gives you the best chance of turning the situation around.

Epilogue

When it comes to managing conflict with people, the smart person has a strategy ready to handle the situation. The foolish person seeks to avoid it altogether.

117

See Conflict or Disagreement as an Opportunity

One strategy for managing conflict is to see it as an opportunity, whether to gain better clarity, straighten out a misunderstanding, correct a miscommunication, or simply to know where you stand with someone.

Conflict can actually be the catalyst for moving forward. People who avoid conflict or confrontation usually take the duck-and-dodge approach, which is a journey of constant detours around the real issue—and missed opportunities to resolve it.

> ### Assignment
>
> The next time you encounter conflict with someone, stop and ask this one magic question: "Can you help me understand from where you are coming?" Then listen to understand. You will be amazed at the results.

We have all seen this in the workplace: two coworkers who disagree, but no one really remembers why. Likely, the current relationship started due to a misunderstanding of intentions, or a miscommunication, and the situation has festered and infected every interaction they have. Because neither extended the olive branch of understanding to the other, they have found themselves in a downward spiral of egotistical pride and unresolved misunderstandings.

But when you accept the conflict at hand and ride it out on the high road, it can present you with a breakthrough. For example, if your finance colleague sees a situation one way, and you see it another, you both have an opportunity: *You* have an opportunity to learn from where the other person is coming; your finance colleague may be trying to tighten expenditures in your division—and others across the board—so the company can avoid layoffs. In reality, your colleague is looking out for you and others.

When you approach conflict with such an attitude of learning and understanding, you have an opportunity to turn it around, and reshape it into something valuable.

Epilogue

Conflict and confrontation can be catalysts for moving forward in a given situation.

118

See Rough Starts as an Opportunity

Yeah, we've all done it—stepped in it right out of the gate, put our foot in our mouth, said something insensitive or just flat-out wrong.

When this happens with others we've known for a while, and with whom we've built a rapport in time, we get a margin of forgiveness. But when it happens with people we're meeting for the first time, it often results in a rough start.

Assignment

Have you had a rough start with someone recently—a week ago, a month ago? Don't let any more time pass. Go find the person and smooth over the situation.

Some people let their pride or embarrassment rule them in these situation. These folks practice avoidance behavior; they avoid the person thereafter.

This is the wrong approach. When things start out rocky, go ask for a mulligan—a do-over. This doesn't mean you have to grovel or supplicate yourself. Your approach could be as simple as, "Sorry about what I said earlier. I clearly wasn't in my right mind." Most people will laugh; if not outwardly, they will on the inside. Why? Because we've all been there; we've all done that.

Epilogue

Circling back to smooth over a rough start shows you have integrity and courage.

119

Breathe!

Researchers have found that, when your adrenaline is pumping, your brain gets less oxygen, and that impairs your ability to reason.

Assignment

Next time you find your dander up, stop talking and breathe, breathe, breathe!

When you find yourself in a conflict situation, stop talking and take a deep breath. In fact, take several.

The simple act of breathing will get oxygen flowing to your brain cells, and will put them back into action, so you can stop yourself from saying or doing something you may regret later.

Ever done that? Been in a conversation that was going south and later thought back to what you said? Did you ask yourself: "What was I thinking?" Well, science tells us that if your adrenaline kicked in, you probably weren't thinking—at least not clearly.

Breathing helps you get your fight-or-flight response back in check, and returns control to the thinking part of your brain.

> **Epilogue**
>
> *The simple act of breathing will get oxygen flowing to your brain cells and help you regain control of your thinking.*

120

Give Yourself a Pep Talk

Okay, be careful with this one. You don't want to be caught having a one-way conversation out loud. But talking yourself down from a conflict situation can help you regain focus.

Assignment

Think of positive things to say about each of your coworkers when conflict should arise, and have those statements ready in your mind to remind yourself with every calming, deep breath you take.

While you're taking all those deep breaths recommended in Idea 119, add in some self meditation, so to speak. Quietly tell yourself with each breath: "I can handle this. He's just trying to be understood. He's just trying to be heard. I can give him that."

Giving yourself a pep talk, along with resupplying oxygen to your brain through deep breathing, helps you control yourself—and that's the only person in a conflict *you can* control.

> ### Epilogue
> *Self-talk helps you get control of yourself, the only person you can control in a disagreement.*

121

Have the Difficult Conversations Beforehand

One of the best ways to manage conflict is to head it off, and resolve tense issues before they become full-blown conflicts. You can do that by *having* difficult conversations—those conversations you avoid, and really want to just forget about.

> ### *Assignment*
> Take stock of your current work relationships. Is there one that seems tense, as though it could be heading for a conflict? If so, take action today.

Yes, there is a time to let sleeping dogs lie. But when you're getting signs that a relationship is souring or heading toward rough times, you need to step it up and have that uncomfortable conversation.

Now, you're not looking to bring a situation to a boil. Simple acknowledgement of the mounting tension can be enough to break the ice with someone, and get a productive dialog going.

For example, you could begin with, "It seems like we're not seeing eye to eye on this, and I want to get some better clarity on your viewpoint." These words can strengthen any existing rapport, and build it within a new relationship.

144

The point is to make the effort, take the first step, and broach the subject. You'll find this to be a more powerful approach than you imagine.

> ### Epilogue
> *When you're getting signs that a relationship is turning sour, or moving toward a full-blown conflict, head it off with a calm, preemptive conversation to clear the air.*

122

Handle Conflict One-on-One

Hey, look, it's *your* problem. Not everyone else's. Got a problem with someone else? Don't like the way she treats you? Has she been dealing you dirt behind your back?

> ### Assignment
> Consider all the times someone went to your boss about something you did or a decision you made. How did that make you feel?

So deal with it! Directly. Don't go to your boss. Don't go to her boss. Don't run around telling everyone else in the office. Make your first stop a conversation directly with the individual involved. If you do that correctly, you'll have a chance to re-create the relationship in a positive way. If you go to your boss, or the other's boss, or tell others around the office, you'll just make the situation worse and likely destroy any chance you had at fixing this problem yourself and coming out of it with a positive solution.

Handling it one-on-one does not involve anything other than direct discussion about the problem. Do it in private, with just the two of you present. Approach the other with the problem objectively, and seek a common solution—one that can benefit both of you. Involving others simply complicates the issue with other relationships.

> **Epilogue**
> *Remember to deal with it yourself and look for the win-win solution.*

123

Having Your Say Doesn't Mean Always Having Your Way

Young professionals usually have the most difficult time with this, sometimes to the point of resenting their boss or more senior-level coworkers. But more experienced professionals become somewhat immune in time to the fact that having your say does not mean having your way.

> **Assignment**
>
> When you know you are going to have a chance to have your say, determine ahead of time, based on conservative expectations, what will be a success for you when all is said and done.

Go into situations with reasonable expectations: Just because you're being given a voice on an issue doesn't mean your ideas will be accepted. A good way to put this into perspective, and avoid letting these incidents deflate your confidence, is to think of a baseball batting average. If you get more than 30 percent of your ideas accepted during your tenure with a particular organization, you're doing well. And those who have learned to master the art of listening and learning are likely to bat a 70-percent average.

The point is to have reasonable expectations that being heard doesn't always translate into things going your way. If you understand this, you will head off disagreements and potential conflict based on your own personal view of reality—because your reality may not be the same as someone else's.

Epilogue

Have reasonable expectations of people and situations, and remember that having your say with someone doesn't mean you will get your way.

124

Learn to Eat Crow

Another way to handle conflict effectively is to admit when you're wrong—quickly. People who admit they are wrong win our respect far

Assignment

Do you have any overdue crow to eat? If so, get busy doing it. The longer you wait, the more damage you will do.

more often than people who just can't bring themselves to do it. But there are times when you have to cast off your pride and face the fact that you just messed up with someone.

When that happens, a quick but sincere apology is in order. And we do mean *quick*. In fact, you should follow the age-old marriage advice of making amends before the sun sets. Use the COB code for the office: Apologize before Close of Business.

Eating crow is as simple as telling the person, "Jack, I'm sorry about earlier today. I overreacted. I hope we can get let bygones be bygones on this one and move forward."

However, if you cut someone down in front of a group, you'll have to eat a bigger helping of crow. That means you will have to apologize privately *and* at the next group gathering. See why we recommend allowing others to save face (Idea 94)?

Epilogue

When you're wrong, cast off your pride and quickly apologize. You will regain the injured party's respect for you.

125

Bring the Peace Pipe

When you sense that tension might be brewing between you and someone else, make a peace offering. But note that these should be given only with the most sincere intentions— not for the purposes of sucking

Assignment

What peace offerings can you make today? Identify them and make them happen.

up. Again, people can smell insincerity a mile away.

So what are peace offerings? They are small gestures, such as a humorous article you know the other person will like, an offer to make a run for mid-morning coffee or lunch; a surprise, mid-afternoon delivery of the person's favorite brand of soda; or strawberries from your garden. The list could go on and on.

The point is to commit random acts of kindness, with the strict intention of being helpful and trustworthy.

> **Epilogue**
>
> *When tension is building between you and a coworker, offer a peace pipe.*

126

Break Bread

When you're sensing that a relationship could be better, find a reason to break bread with the other party. There is something about food that just brings people together

> **Assignment**
>
> Identify two relationships you need to nurture, either to build or to maintain, and plan lunch dates with those individuals.

and softens their defenses. Sales professionals know this technique very well, and use it weekly, and, in some cases, daily.

Breaking bread is as simple as going to lunch together, or to breakfast, or for after-hours tapas. Food relaxes people and creates an informal setting. Just pick a place that has a low-key atmosphere and is relatively quiet. Nothing kills an opportunity to break bread productively like a noisy, high-energy restaurant.

When you do sit down to break bread, remember to go with the flow. In fact, it's better not to have a mental agenda to accomplish at the meal, other than getting face time with the person.

And remember: Breaking bread is not just for relationships on the fritz; it's also a great way to connect with people and get to know them. In fact, it's a great idea to plan individual bread-breaking "sessions" every month with a handful of people with whom you're working to build rapport.

> ### Epilogue
> *There is something about food that brings people together, and softens their defenses. To help smooth conflict with someone, break bread together.*

127

Fight Fair

When conflict leads to confrontation, fight fair! Some people escalate conflict to confrontation in a matter of seconds, so there could be instances when you find yourself with no time to head off tangling antlers with the office hothead, for example. But even when that happens, you have a responsibility to fight fair.

Assignment

Think of times when someone did not treat you fairly in a disagreement. What were the other person's actions or behaviors? Think about how you would have handled that situation if you had been that person.

Fighting fair means you have to stick to the issue at hand, argue the facts of the matter, keep your comments neutral, and keep it between you and the other person.

Okay, we'll break it down: Stick to the issue at hand. That means no dragging up past transgressions of the other party. You must stay focused on the matter that needs to be resolved immediately—and that's all!

Also, focus on the *facts* of the matter. Set your personal biases or dislikes about the person to the side, and keep to the points that are in disagreement. You'll also want to watch any general statements, too, such as: "Kate, you always do this!" That's not only unfair, it's also immature.

And, finally, keep the matter between you and the other person, if the situation allows. Some people will argue an issue openly in a meeting, which makes everyone uncomfortable and often does irreparable damage to the relationship.

Keeping it between the two of you is simple. Ask to take the conversation "offline" for another time, discuss it calmly later, and resist the temptation to talk about it with others in the office—or tattle to the boss, if the other party is a coworker.

Fighting fair also means giving the other person the benefit of the doubt whenever you can. Remember: Most people are working from good intentions. Let that thought lead your comments when you find yourself in confrontation.

Epilogue
When conflict turns to confrontation, remember to fight fair!

128

Be Mindful of Your Thoughts; They Can Be a Path to the Dark Side

Star Wars fans will find this statement familiar. Yes, we pay tribute here to the wisdom of Master Yoda, who is forever warning his Jedi pupils that their thoughts are the seeds of their actions.

Well, the little green guy is right! What you put in your

> ## *Assignment*
> Check your thoughts. Are they based on fair thinking? Do they give others the benefit of the doubt?

head becomes what you sow over time. If you walk around with negative and critical thoughts about your coworkers, that will be the nature of your relationships.

People can pick up on a vibe from you, and they know if you have less-than-favorable thoughts about them. Even Christian author and motivational speaker Joyce Meyers warns that negative thoughts can attract negative outcomes.

People can usually pick up on a negative vibe based on nonverbal communication, such as body language, gestures, and tone, which are all founded on what's running through your head. But when you give people the benefit of the doubt and believe they are working from their best intentions, you can counter those negative thoughts.

So, let go. Assume the best of people, until they give you clear and consistent reason not to.

Epilogue
What you put in your head about people becomes how you interact with them in time.

129

Don't Take Things Personal

We know, we know—a lot easier said than done! But it's a good policy to practice. There are two situations you need to consider

when working to not take things personal. The first is your ego; the second is the other person's ego.

Because you can only control you, let's start there. If you want to be taken seriously, then you have to have some tough skin, and be able to know the difference between someone criticizing your ideas and finding fault with you personally.

Challenging your ideas and decisions is par for the working world, so you need to accept it. We are all challenged and questioned from time to time, and some people are challenged daily. Even your CEO gets pushback regularly.

The second situation you may have to deal with is that of the office bully. People who make an issue personal and try to drag you down usually don't have a good argument for their position to begin with. That's why they try to divert the issue and make it about you. But it isn't.

So what do you do when someone takes the conversation to a personal level? There are two options, depending on the situation. First, calmly and politely tell the person the issue is not about you; it's about X project. A more firm approach may be necessary though, such as, "Joe, I'm happy to have a productive conversation with you about project X. If you want to calm down and talk about this later today, I'll gladly do so."

This firm approach will let the person know you've set boundaries, and he needs to respect them if he wants to work with you.

Epilogue

When you find yourself in the midst of a tense situation, sort out the seeds of truth that can help you, and let the rest of it just roll off your back.

130

Don't Make Things Personal

While you're working on not taking things personal, also be sure not to *make* things personal.

When you make personal digs at others

Assignment

Think about a coworker who makes situations personal. Do people truly respect him or her?

when conflict arises, you just drag yourself down, and you help the other person garner sympathy from office colleagues. This type of behavior shows your maturity—or immaturity—level.

In tense situations, you have to work even harder to practice the Golden Rule, and make a concentrated effort to show others respect. That means you have to pull out all the tools, such as listening, seeking to understand, controlling your thoughts, breathing, and so on.

Particularly control your breathing and your thoughts. The breathing exercise (Idea 119) will help you keep your brain from going on autopilot, and will help you keep control of your thoughts and reactions.

And it's important to realize that making things personal when conflict arises is exactly that: a reaction. Yet it's a reaction that can, and will, do permanent damage. Don't let that happen. Don't make situations personal.

Epilogue

Making personal digs at others when situations get tense only drags you down and makes you look bad.

131

He Who Keeps His Mouth Shut, Keeps His Life

Silence is golden—and never more so than when conflict arises. The old adage that recommends that you listen twice as much as you talk is absolutely true in tense circumstances.

Assignment

Read on to Idea 141 for a good technique on what to say during tense situations.

When it comes to talking during conflict, take the less-is-more approach. This is particularly true if the other party is the boss, the office hothead, or someone with whom you don't have rapport yet.

In fact, the more you talk in a conflict situation, the more you run the risk of saying something that could be career limiting—especially if the disagreement is with the boss.

Be careful, however, not to interpret this advice as a suggestion that you should be sullen or obstinate. That can get you into trouble, too. The point is to keep your intentions focused on resolving the issue in a way that keeps the relationship from going south. Keeping your ears and mind open, and your mouth closed for the most part, is a better approach than pushing your case in the face of conflict.

Epilogue

When it comes to talking during conflict, take the less-is-more approach: The less said, the better.

132

Dial Down the Volume

Sometimes disagreements can be swiftly cooled if we just speak more softly. But usually, next to our adrenaline and blood pressure levels, the volume of our voices is the first thing to rise when we disagree with someone.

Be cognizant of this. Lower your voice at the first sign of tension. Speaking more softly can send the message that you're not a threat.

Assignment

In the next few days, observe people interacting. Who in your office speaks softly, but articulately in tense discussions? What effect does that person have on the outcome of the conversation?

It can also calm your own internal system, reducing your adrenaline levels, and allowing your brain to get more oxygen—which helps you think and process information more clearly.

In short, a softer approach can be more effective in tense situations than sheer force.

> **Epilogue**
> *Fiery discussions can be cooled quickly if you just speak more softly.*

133

Watch Your Body Language—It Speaks Volumes

Not only do your words and voice speak volumes in a disagreement, but so do your body language and tone. In fact, these are usually more damaging than the words you use—we forget that more than 80 percent of our communication with others is nonverbal.

> **Assignment**
>
> Ask a trusted colleague to watch your body language when you interact with someone with whom you're having tension, and ask him to give you feedback on what that body language is saying.

That's right! The vast majority of what you say never comes out of your mouth, but it's on display for all to see. For example, if you start to doodle on your notepad while someone is talking, you send the clear message that you don't value what that person says. Or, if you talk on top of someone, cutting her off midsentence, you send the message that you believe she is inferior to you.

Some of the obvious offenses are rolling your eyes, smirking, folding your arms across your chest, or putting your hands on your hips.

Be careful of the message you're sending with your body language. Your words could be saying one thing, but your gestures speaking much louder.

157

Epilogue

More than 80 percent of what you say is through your body language and tone. Yep, that means the vast majority of what you say never comes out of your mouth, but speaks volumes nonetheless.

134

Give People Space

When situations become heated, sometimes all people need is a little space, a little time to cool off.

If you're someone who needs closure on a

Assignment

Think about a time when you needed a few days to cool off. Did you have a better outlook on things afterward?

---

tense situation, you may need to wait a day or so and apply one of the relationship tips mentioned previously, such as bringing the peace pipe, or breaking bread with someone. When people need space, timing can make the difference between a mended fence and salt in the wound.

Remember: If you're feeling bad about the situation, it's likely the other person is too. And she may just need a day or two to hide out and lick her wounds—and recover from her own embarrassment about how she also handled the situation.

Don't let the silence bother you too much, but, if the person is still giving you the cold shoulder after a few days, you'll need to muster up the courage to sit down with him one on one, and smooth things over—as much as is appropriate. You should not extend yourself further than the situation warrants.

There is no shame in extending the olive branch. It only shows that you're open to working things out, and maintaining a productive relationship.

> ### Epilogue
> *When conflict arises, some people just need time to cool off. Give them space to do so.*

135

What Goes Over the Devil's Back, Always Comes Under His Belly

This is just a southern way of saying "what goes around, comes around." If you mistreat someone in some way, or disrespect her, you will reap what you sow. You can call it karma or po-

> ### Assignment
> Reread ideas 85 through 99. These are lessons that never get old, because you will use them again and again throughout your life.

etic justice. It really doesn't matter; you just want to make sure whatever you sow with others is going to come back to you in a good way.

When we hurt others by not allowing them to save face, making conflicts personal, maligning them, gossiping, or tattling about them to the boss, they will not forget it. And it will affect their judgment about you, and how cooperative they will be in working with you in the future. It's very likely they will also tell others about your behavior.

If you want what they say to be something of which you can be proud, then sow seeds of collaboration, cooperation, encouragement, fairness, honor, and consistency. These make up the soil in which good relationships are grown.

Epilogue

What goes around, comes around, so make sure what you sow with others comes back to you in a good way.

136

There Is No Right or Wrong

There are times when we like to think that we're right and someone else is wrong. But there are never absolutes when people disagree. Sometimes we like to convince ourselves there are, but that's wrong in itself.

Assignment

Challenge yourself this week to inquire about someone else's viewpoint you have previously considered wrong.

No viewpoint is without scrutiny, question, or challenge. In fact, all viewpoints are exactly that: a view of where someone sits in terms of life experience and knowledge. And we all come from different experiences, backgrounds, and beliefs.

Holding to the conclusion that your viewpoint is right and someone else's is wrong is a missed opportunity to expand your horizons and see an issue from a different angle. In short, it's a missed opportunity to learn, and to understand, and a missed opportunity to find common ground.

So let go of any stubborn hold you have of right and wrong viewpoints, and accept them for what they are—simply a perspective from which someone has traveled so far in life.

Epilogue

Holding to the conclusion that your viewpoint is right and someone else's is wrong is a missed opportunity to expand your horizons.

137

Winner Never Takes All

If your approach to conflict has been to win at all costs, then that cost could be very high for you in the long run.

We've all met them—the people who have to win the debate, trump the argument, and put down all opposition for the sheer enjoyment of being right.

And just as we learn when we drive in traffic, you may have the right-of-way to make that left turn, but the guy speeding toward you may not care—and you end up with the honor of being dead right. Wow! How useful!

Winning at all costs is a short-term and shortsighted strategy. Sure, you might win in the heat of battle, but you could leave a lot of carnage on the battlefield, and wounds that will never heal with some people.

In short, the winner does not take all—but risks losing a lot in the long run.

Assignment

When you find yourself in disagreement, concede where you can concede. Give on points you can give on. And work with the long-term, greater good in mind.

> **Epilogue**
> *Winning at all costs in a conflict is a shortsighted strategy.*

138

Fight for the Relationship

When you fight for the future of a working relationship, you often have to fight your own demons, your own inclinations, and your own temptations to win in the short term. You have to fight the urge to beat someone mentally into seeing things your way.

Assignment

When preparing for a discussion that could result in conflict, consider how you want the relationship to be in the long term. Then determine actions and responses that will help you achieve that goal.

When you experience difficult discussions with others, always keep the future in mind. Ask yourself this series of questions: What do you want that relationship to ultimately be? How can that relationship ultimately benefit you, your work, and your organization? Does a short-term win get you there, or is living to fight another day a better strategy?

Those who are effective in negotiation and dispute resolutions will tell you to consider your end goal with every action you take. If that action will undermine your goals, then it's not a card you want to play. Discard it and choose another that will help you win in the long run.

To achieve a long-term victory out of conflict, you have to reach for the win-win. It's the only way to play the relationship game.

> ### Epilogue
> *When you experience difficult discussions with others, always keep the future of that relationship in mind.*

139

Get Clear

Another quick and easy way to head off conflict is to make sure you understand the situation.

Ever gone all reactive on someone only to find out later that you completely misunderstood

> ### Assignment
> Make it part of your personal policy not to act in a disagreement until you're sure you have the facts; without them, you can't be sure a disagreement truly exists.

the situation or his intentions? Ever let your biases or personal dislikes of someone make you think the worst of him—only to be proven wrong later?

Then who had egg on her face? Did you feel that your credibility slipped a few notches? If so, you were right to feel that way. And we've all done it. The trick is to avoid it altogether.

So, before you head off down the warpath after someone, make sure you have the facts. And the best technique for gathering that information is to go to the person you're about to scalp—but leave the tomahawk in your office and bring the peace pipe instead (Idea 125).

> ### Epilogue
> *Before you head off down the warpath after someone, make sure you have the facts.*

140

Present, Don't Persuade

One of the most common mistakes we make in a disagreement is to convince ourselves that we must persuade the other person to see our point of view.

But all we really need to do is lay out the facts or circumstances. Though people are first and foremost emotional creatures, their emotions are guided by rationality and reason— for the most part.

Assignment

Put this tip to the test. Identify one issue about which you disagree with someone, and approach him on it. Just lay out the facts, without stacking the deck in your favor, and see what result you get. If the person meets you halfway, then you've made progress, and you've found a more effective way to manage conflict.

When you lay out the facts of a situation—in a calm and collected manner—you appeal to people's sense of reason. And you demonstrate that you respect their ability to assess the situation with good judgment.

Persuading people, on the other hand, can come off as manipulative. It can send the message that they're not sensible enough to assess the facts, or that they're not capable of making a good decision and have to be given passionate direction.

To avoid sending this message, change your tactic. Simply lay out the circumstances or facts of why you have come to your position on a matter, and then give people space—and time—to consider them.

You will be pleasantly surprised by the results. You may not get agreement on every point, but it's more than likely the person will at least meet you halfway. Many times that is all you can ask.

> ### Epilogue
> *When you don't see eye-to-eye with someone, change your tactic and present facts to support your point of view, instead of trying to convince or persuade.*

141

Ask, Don't Tell

Okay, say you find yourself in what appears to be a deteriorating conversation, and you can feel the tension growing.

Quickly check yourself. Are you doing all the talking? Are you working hard to have your point of view heard? Are you attempting to persuade

> ### Assignment
> Recall a time when you saw a situation go from bad to worse. Were you doing a lot of talking, telling the other person your viewpoint, working to persuade him to see yours? How might being ask-assertive have helped in that situation?

someone to your way of doing things? If you find yourself doing any of these, stop! Take a breath, and immediately change your approach to being ask-assertive.

What's that, you ask? Well, it's an approach that allows you to still assert yourself, but in a way that's more palatable to the other party because you ask questions, instead of telling the person what you think.

Your questions can be to clarify, or to softly challenge. For example, "Am I understanding that we're going to delay the project for another month?" Or, when challenging, you could say, "Have we considered what could happen if we take that approach?" Or try something such as, "But wouldn't it be better for all parties involved if the project was delayed for only two weeks, instead of a full month?"

In short, being ask-assertive helps you to learn more about from where the person is coming, and gives her the chance to come to conclusions on her own. When you become ask-assertive, you can still get your point across without persuading, convincing, or dominating.

Epilogue

Being ask-assertive helps you to learn more about from where the person is coming, and gives her the chance to come to conclusions on her own.

142

Look for Middle Ground

The best way to resolve a disagreement is to find middle ground to meet the person halfway.

Finding middle ground is the key to creating a win-win in a disagreement. And you want to always strive for the

Assignment

Think of issues you're dealing with right now. Where is your point of middle ground in those situations?

win-win. That way you and the other person both walk away feeling as though you've gotten something you wanted.

The best way to find middle ground is to ask questions of the person—to be ask-assertive. A simple question to kick off the conversation could be: "Tom, what would you see as success on this project?" From Tom's answer, you gain insight into where you can meet him halfway—where you can establish middle ground.

And there is always an opportunity for you to give enough to help the other person give a little, too. In fact, most people will back off of a hardline position when they see the other person is willing to be flexible.

Epilogue

Finding middle ground with someone helps you to create a win-win for all involved.

143

Start From a Point of Commonality

What do we have in common? That's the first question you want to ask yourself when tension raises its ugly head in a working relationship.

Why? Because starting from a point of agreement, or commonality, helps you and the other person get focused on where you're alike, instead of focusing your thoughts on where you're different.

Assignment

Bite the bullet and make a list of what you and your office nemesis have in common, and what you both seem to agree on. Then work from those points to improve your relationship.

In fact, most people throughout the world are more alike than different, regardless of geography, culture, or ethnicity. But we tend to focus on what's different, and that's where most of our difficulties with people start.

So, think about what you and your nemesis have in common. Are you both passionate about your company? Do you each have a strong work ethic? Are you both bright?

Are these traits about yourself that you respect? Then couldn't you also respect them about the other person, and use them as a launching pad for a better relationship?

> **Epilogue**
> *What do we have in common? That's the first question you should ask yourself when you experience a difficult relationship with someone.*

144

Some Nuts Are Worth Cracking

No, we're not giving you permission to think of your office nemesis as a nut! Here we're talking about hanging with those difficult relationships; not giving up at the first sign of trouble and throwing in the towel.

> **Assignment**
> Challenge yourself to crack one office nut.

We do this too often. We write people off at the first sign of difficulty. Sometimes these people have hard exteriors, making it difficult to understand them. Or they are people who seem to dislike us for some unknown reason.

With these folks it could be just a matter of being patient, having diligence, and getting to know the person one interaction at a time. It could be quite a while—months or even years—before we start to see these people warming up to us and our ideas.

But these can also end up being some of the best and most long-lasting relationships we ever develop. So, the next time you encounter the office grump, or the office bully, remember to take your experience with him one day at a time, and to keep working to get past those hard exteriors to the person he is on the inside. You might be surprised to find diamonds in the rough.

Epilogue
The office nut could really be a diamond in the rough.

145

Put the "Moose on the Table"

Sometimes we have to do this when we have difficult relationships; we have to put the moose on the table, which means being straight-up, direct, getting the issue out in the open. Some people call this "kicking the elephant out of the room," or just drawing a line in the sand. Whatever idiom you choose is not important, but taking a stand and airing out an issue is. Have you learned that a colleague is bad-mouthing you around the office? Is someone spreading gossip and rumors about you?

Assignment
If you find you need to put the moose on the table with someone, read ideas 85 through 143 again.

Though you want to use the techniques in this book to help you, you will find times when you will need to approach these folks and put the moose on the table.

Of course, that should be done one-on-one, and always with professional courtesy. But if someone is spreading damaging rumors, gossip, or outright lies about you, then you need to make your stand and set boundaries. And you may need to take this one up with the boss, but only after you've calmly and politely addressed the situation one-on-one with the instigator.

So, what how do you begin a conversation such as that? Simple, with something similar to this: "Jane, there are some disturbing rumors that have reached me, and I've been told you are at the root of them. I hope this is just a misunderstanding. Can you tell me if you said these things about me?"

It really doesn't matter how the person answers. By merely making her aware you have her number, she will think twice in the future.

Some people forget that their companies can be liable for employees' statements that lead to defamation of character and slander. You are within your rights to ask someone to cool it when he's stepped over the line.

Epilogue
You are within your rights to put the moose on the table when someone crosses the line and defames your character or reputation.

146

Pick Your Battles

You'll be pretty worn out, and friendless, if you try to fight every battle that comes your way on the relationship front. In fact, people who try to fight every battle are often seen as reactive and extremist, and are rarely taken seriously.

But the wise among us know that people make mistakes, they have general human failings, and the wise know that we have to let bygones be

> ### Assignment
>
> Ask yourself if you let petty relationship issues keep you drained. If so, then you might be taking on too many battles.

bygones many times in our relationships with people.

If you take a live-and-let-live approach to dealing with people, you will find that they will give the same to you. Let the petty go, let it roll off your back, and save your energy for the bigger things that can bring real meaning to your life.

Not only will this help you stay balanced, but it will also make people more apt to forgive and forget quickly when you mess up yourself—and you will, from time to time.

> ### Epilogue
> *Live and let live whenever you can. People will pay you the same margin of forgiveness along the way.*

147

Mend Fences

If you make mistakes in dealing with people, be quick to acknowledge and correct them. For example, if someone has asked you to keep something confidential, and you let the cat out of the bag, make a beeline to that person's office to apologize.

Do not let another minute set on that type of situation. Mistakes that erode people's trust in you must be corrected immediately.

If the mistake is just a simple mishap or uninten-

> ### Assignment
>
> Do some relationship housecleaning. Have you made any mistakes you need to confess and correct? If so, get busy today mending those fences.

tional error, take care of it at the first opportunity—which generally means *finding* an opportunity within the next 24 hours. Track down the person, bring the peace pipe (Idea 125), and dive right in to an apology.

And do not be glib about it with a cavalier comment such as "my bad." Be sincere, be authentic, and be serious about the situation—especially if your actions can affect the future of your relationship with the other person.

Epilogue
If you make mistakes that can erode people's trust in you, immediately take action to correct the situation—an apology is a good place to start.

148

Forgive Yourself for Failings

So, you messed up. Have you taken the steps outlined in this book, such as mending fences, eating crow, offering a peace pipe, and breaking bread?

If so, then all you can do is get on with your life. You've done all you can to correct the situation. Sometimes we have to just give people space to get over something—and we have to forgive ourselves, too.

Beating yourself up over and over about a

> ## Assignment
> Take stock. Are you beating yourself up about something you tried sincerely to correct? If so, write a phrase to describe the situation on a piece of paper, then run it through the office shredder, and let go of it in your mind from this moment forward.

situation only continues to keep the situation alive, not only in your mind, but in the other person's mind as well. And it puts you at risk of making the same mistake again.

If you've apologized, tried to restore the trust in the relationship, and changed your behavior, then you've done your part. You've adequately taken responsibility, and that's something in which you can find honor.

We all mess up with each other from time to time. When you mess up, do the right thing, then forgive yourself and move on.

> ### Epilogue
> *If you've done all you can to take responsibility for a failing regarding a relationship, then find honor in that, and forgive yourself.*

149

Forgive Others as Well

Just as you have to forgive yourself for your own failings, you also have to forgive others when they fail you.

And others will fail you—both intentionally and unintentionally. The latter is much easier to forgive, if we know someone did not mean to hurt us. But what about those who fully intended to do us harm?

> ### Assignment
> Are you holding a grudge against someone? If so, ask yourself if that energy and effort is moving you forward or holding you in the past.

You may need to put the moose on the table (Idea 145) with these folks, but when that's said and done, then you have to get over it and get on with your life.

Forgiving others requires you to travel the high road. And sometimes that's a hard road to take. But for the sake of your own integrity and sanity, it's an important journey for you.

With people who fail us intentionally, you have to stand up and be the bigger person, and accept the fact that these folks have some growing to do. As long as you don't let their shortcomings become your own, you can use the situation as a learning experience and a growth opportunity for your own maturity.

> ### Epilogue
> *Forgiving others requires you to journey down the high road.*

150

Be the First to Offer the Olive Branch—or the Peace Pipe

Ever felt as though you were in a stalemate with someone with whom you've had a dust-up? It's very likely she would like to put the situation behind her

too. In most cases, people avoid each other after a wrangling because they are both afraid the other person will either do him more injury, or reject his overtures of apology.

Be the first to make the overture anyway. Yeah, yeah, the George Castanzas of the world will tell you this is a mistake, that you have "hand" and you should keep it. But we all know George was not known for his people skills.

So, dig out the olive branch—or a peace pipe—and start that long walk down the company corridors to deliver it. Sometimes you don't even need to say anything. Getting things back on track with someone might be as simple as dropping off a can of their favorite soda—without any pomp or circumstance.

In short, find a way either directly or indirectly—depending on how bad the dust-up was—to be the first to mend fences. Your efforts will very likely be rewarded.

Epilogue

Be the first to make an overture of peace when relationships hit a rough spot.

151

Every Difficult Relationship Has Lessons

As much as difficult relationships can give us heartburn and sleepless nights, they are an essential part of our growth as people.

Difficult relationships not only teach us a lot about others, but

> ### *Assignment*
>
> The next time you run into a difficult personality to deal with, view it as a test of your people skills. Accept the challenge and persevere!

they also teach us more about ourselves—such as what pushes our buttons and what boundaries we will not go beyond.

In essence, they are the sandpaper that hones and polishes us. And sometimes the powers that be put these people in our way to teach us lessons and help us grow to new levels of strength and maturity—and forgiveness.

And difficult relationships—difficult people in particular— give us practice in putting our people skills to the test. It's been said that it's easy to be an angel when no one ruffles your feathers. But difficult relationships are the litmus test for how evolved we really are in dealing with people, and managing ourselves in the process.

Epilogue

Difficult relationships are like sandpaper. They hone and polish us.

Index

A

Actions, principles and, 36

Adrenaline, 142-143

Aggression, 70, 87

Alessandra, Dr. Tony, 32

Anniversaries, remembering, 123-124

Apologizing, 147-148, 173

Asian cultures, 113

Ask-assertiveness, 165-166

Asking questions, 104-105

Assertiveness, 70

Assumptions, 64-65

Attention, undivided, 100-101

Authenticity, 47-48

Awareness, social, 21

B

Bank account, emotional, 124-125

Battles, choosing your, 171-172

Being dismissive, 61-62

Being positive, 58-59

Being present, 101-102

Being reactive, 87, 88-89

Believing in others, 71-72

Birthdays, remembering, 123-124

Body language, 94, 157-158

Boundaries, 38-40

Breaking bread, 149-150

Breathing, 142-143, 154-155

Bribery, 63-64
Bully, office, 155
Burnout, people, 124-125

C

Caring, 18-19
Carlin, George, 42
Carnegie, Dale, 17, 94
Celebrations, 122-123
Character, 46-47
Character, defamation of, 170
Cheerleading others, 118-119
Choosing your battles, 171-172
Commonality, point of, 167-168
Communication, face-to-face, 91-92
Communication, nonverbal, 82
Compassion, 110-111
Compassionate honesty, 110
Complaint, 59-60
Condescension, 62-63
Conflict, 136-142, 144-146, 150-151, 155-156, 163-164
Confrontation, 141
Connotation, 55-56
Consistency, 59
Contempt, 60

Courage, 142
Covey, Stephen, 36
Creator personality style, 76, 79, 80
Criticism, 59-60
Crow, eating, 147-148
Cynics, 66-67

D

Defamation of character, 170
Defensiveness, 60
Denotation, 55-56
Difficult relationships, 176-177
Directness, 167-170
Director personality style, 76, 79, 80
Disagreements, 140
Discernment, 52-53
Dismissive, being, 61-62
Dominance, 87
Domineering, 68, 87-88
Doolittle, Eliza, 28
Doubt, benefit of the, 30-31

E

Eastern cultures, 113-114
Eating crow, 147-148

Edifying, 109-110, 129-130

E-mail, 90, 92, 93-94

Emerson, Ralph Waldo, 96

Emotion, 94-95

Emotional bank account, 124-125

Emotional equity, 95-96

Emotional intelligence (EQ), 17-18, 97-98

Emotionally charged words, 55-56

Encouragement, 72, 114-116

Encouraging quotations, 116

Encouraging words, 116

Events, social, 135-136

Expectations, 34, 35, 138-139, 146-147

Eye contact, 99-100

F

Face-to-face communication, 91-92

Failings, 172-173

Fear, 67, 89

Fences, mending, 171-172, 175

Fighting fair, 150-151

Fight-or-flight syndrome, 143

Flaws, 47

Food, 149-150

Forgiveness, 172-174

Formal networks, 21

Four Horsemen, the, 59-60

Friends, 96-97

G

Generations, 46

Genuine, 40-41

Goals, helping others achieve their, 119-120

Golden Rule, the, 15, 25, 30, 31, 32, 54, 78, 154

Goldman, Daniel, 17

Gossip, 60-61

Growth, 71

H

Handling conflict correctly, 136-142

Helping others achieve their goals, 119-120

Helping others be heard, 111-112

Helping others be understood, 112-113

Honesty, 110-111, 127-128

Humility, 43

Humor, sense of, 42-43

I

Inferiority, 82-83, 84
Informal networks, 21-22
Ingratiating, 27-28
Inspiration, 128-129
Integrity, 48-49, 142
Intelligence, emotional, 17-18, 97-98
Intelligence, social, 15, 19-21, 34
Intentions, 29-30
Interaction, live, 90-92
Intimidation, 84, 89-90

J

Judgment, 30, 106-107, 111

K

Karma, 159-160
Keeping your word, 50-51
Kind words, 58-59

L

Lambert, Dr. Howard, 59-60
Laughing at yourself, 43-44
Listening, 82, 86, 88, 100, 102-103, 115, 137, 155-156

Live interaction, 90-92
Lunch hour, 134-135

M

Manipulation, 63-64
Manning, Peyton, 121
Mending fences, 171-172, 175
Meyers, Joyce, 152
Middle ground, 166-167
Mistakes, 44-45
Motives, 29-30
Myers-Briggs scale, 125-126

N

Names, remembering, 98-99
Need to win, 161-162
Needs, your own, 125-126
Negativity, 65, 152
Networks, 21-22
Nonverbal communication, 82

O

Office bully, 155
Open-mindedness, 108
Opinions, 69, 76, 80, 105-106
Opinions, style vs., 76, 80

Opportunities, mistakes as, 44-45
Others, believing in, 71-72
Overreacting, 67
Oxygen, 142-143

P

Patronization, 62
Peace offerings, 148-149
Peaceful relationships, 72
Peacemakers, 73-74
People break, 131-132
People burnout, 124-125
People skills, 20
Persistence, 168-169
Personal, making things, 154-155
Personal opinions, 105-106
Personality styles, 74-80
Personally, taking things, 153-154
Perspective, 115-116
Persuasion, 164-165
Pessimism, 65-66
Platinum Rule, the, 15-16, 25, 32, 78, 79
Positive, being, 58-59
Present, being, 101-102

Presenting, 164-165
Principle-Centered Leadership, 36
Principles, 36-38, 49
Promises, 50-51
Pygmalian Effect, the, 16, 28-29

Q

Questions, asking, 104-105
Quotations, encouraging, 116

R

Rapport, 20, 35
Reactive, being, 87, 88-89
Reading, 133-134
Reason, 94
Reasonable expectations, 146-147
Recognizing all viewpoints, 160-161
Relationship skill set, 45-46
Relationships, 22-26, 33, 72, 176-177
Relationships, difficult, 176-177
Relationships, peaceful, 72
Remembering birthdays and anniversaries, 123-124

Remembering names, 98-99

Reputation, 46-47

Respect, 25-26, 53-54, 113

Role models, 130-131

Roosevelt, Eleanor, 83

S

Saving face, 113-114

Self-confidence, 34, 89

Self-deprecation, 43-44

Self-doubt, 89

Self-esteem, 83, 85

Sense of humor, 42-43

Seriousness, 41-42

Service, 26-27

Shaw, George Bernard, 28

Shyness, 80-82

Silence, 155-156, 158

Skills, technical, 19-21, 97-98

Slander, 170

Smiling, 82

Social awareness, 21

Social events, 135-136

Social goofs, 44

Social intelligence, 15, 19-21, 34

Solutions, 33

Space, giving, 158-159

Spotlight, 120-121

Star Wars, 152

Stonewalling, 60

Stubbornness, 160

Styles, personality, 74-80

Support group, 126-127

Supporter personality style, 76, 79, 80

T

Talkativeness, 85

Technical skills, 19-21, 97-98

Technology, 90-91

Text messages, 90, 92

"That's Wild," 134-135

Tolerance, 54-55

Tone, 157-158

Trust, 25-26, 49-50

U

Undivided attention, 100-101

V

Viewpoints, recognizing all, 160-161

Voice mail, 90, 92

Voice volume, 156-157

W

Western culture, 114

Williams, Robin, 42

Win, need to, 161-162

Wooden, John, 130-131

Word, keeping your, 50-51

Words, emotionally charged, 55-56

Words, encouraging, 116

Words, kind, 58-59

Y

Yoda, 152

About the Authors

Robert E. Dittmer, APR

Bob Dittmer has more than 35 years of experience in the public relations, marketing, and higher education.

He is currently a faculty member with the Indiana University School of Journalism in Indianapolis, having more than 19 years of experience as an adjunct faculty member with colleges and universities around the country, in both undergraduate and graduate programs. He currently teaches public relations courses, is the director of graduate studies, and also serves as the marketing and retention officer.

Bob has also served as the director of media relations for both an American government organization with responsibilities for all of Europe, and for a major NATO organization with responsibilities for public information worldwide. He has more than 25 years of experience in public relations and advertising agencies, working with a variety of clients in both the business-to-business and business-to-consumer areas. Bob is also the author of *151 Quick Ideas to Manage Your Time* and coauthor of *151 Quick Ideas for Delegating and Decision Making* (with Stephanie McFarland).

Stephanie McFarland, APR

More than 20 years ago, Stephanie McFarland began her management career by supervising employees for her family's business.

Stephanie has managed projects, teams, and departments in multinational, Fortune 500, government, consultancy, and nonprofit organizations within the past 19 years. She has provided public relations counseling to more than 20 clients and employers in the electrical and pharmaceutical industries, as well as others.

Her personal philosophy of management has evolved throughout the years from merely motivating employees "to get the job done" to discovering what makes them tick as well as ways to further develop their current roles.

Stephanie is an adjunct professor for the Indiana University School of Journalism in Indianapolis, where she teaches public relations management courses to undergraduate and graduate students.

151 Quick Ideas to Get New Customers
Jerry R. Wilson ◆ 978-1-56414-830-8

151 Quick Ideas to Inspire Your Staff
Jerry R. Wilson ◆ 978-1-56414-829-2

151 Quick Ideas to Manage Your Time
Robert E. Dittmer ◆ 978-1-56414-899-5

151 Quick Ideas to Recognize and Reward Employees
Ken Lloyd, Ph.D. ◆ 978-1-56414-945-9

151 Quick Ideas for Delegating and Decision Making
Robert E. Dittmer and Stephanie McFarland ◆ 978-1-56414-961-9

151 Quick Ideas to Deal With Difficult People
Carrie Mason-Draffen ◆ 978-1-56414-938-1

151 Quick Ideas for Advertising on a Shoestring
Jean Joachim ◆ 978-1-56414-982-4